Mendez v. Westminster

LANDMARK LAW CASES

AMERICAN SOCIETY

Peter Charles Hoffer

N. E. H. Hull

Series Editors

For a complete list of titles in the series go to www.kansaspress.ku.edu

PHILIPPA STRUM

Mendez v. Westminster

School Desegregation and

Mexican-American Rights

UNIVERSITY PRESS OF KANSAS

Published by the University Press of Kansas (Lawrence, Kansas 66045), which was
organized by the Kansas Board of Regents and is operated and funded by Emporia
State University, Fort Hays State University, Kansas State University, Pittsburg State
University, the University of Kansas, and Wichita State University

Library of Congress Cataloging-in-Publication Data

Strum, Philippa.
Mendez v. Westminster : school desegregation and Mexican-American rights /
Philippa Strum.
p. cm.—(Landmark law cases and American society)
Includes bibliographical references and index.
ISBN 978-0-7006-1718-0 (cloth : alk. paper)
ISBN 978-0-7006-1719-7 (pbk. : alk. paper)
1. Segregation in education—Law and legislation—United States. 2. Discrimination
in education—Law and legislation—United States. 3. Mexican Americans—
Education—United States. 4. Mexican Americans—Legal status, laws, etc.—United
States. 5. Segregation in education—Law and legislation—California—Orange
County. 6. Mexican Americans—Legal status, laws, etc.—California—Orange
County. 7. Méndez, Gonzalo. 8. Westminster School District (Orange County,
Calif.) I. Title. II. Title: Mendez versus Westminster.
KF4155.S77 2010
344.73'07980264--dc21
2009052268

British Library Cataloguing-in-Publication Data is available.

Printed in the United States of America

10 9 8 7 6 5 4 3 2 1

The paper used in this publication is recycled and contains 30 percent postconsumer
waste. It is acid free and meets the minimum requirements of the American National
Standard for Permanence of Paper for Printed Library Materials Z39.48-1992.

For the Red Line Group,
with a smile

CONTENTS

Every student of American history and law knows *Brown v. Board of Education*. Love it or not, it is a constitutional landmark. Few of us—even scholars—knew about *Mendez v. Westminster School District*. That is about to change. Philippa Strum's deeply moving, swiftly paced account of this landmark education law and civil rights case will put it on the map of American history as a precursor to *Brown* and more. *Mendez* did more for Mexican-American schoolchildren than *Brown* did for African-Americans, and the case showed that organization, courage, and persistence in the Mexican-American communities of Orange County, California, could displace the almost casual racism of Anglo-dominated school boards.

Mendez was not argued as a case about racial discrimination. At the time it was brought, *Plessy v. Ferguson* and its pernicious formula still reigned in public school education. All parties agreed that Mexican ancestry, not race (the Mexicans were deemed "white"), was the crux of the matter. But counsel for the many parents who joined in the suit laid the groundwork for a far broader assault on arbitrary classifications and discrimination against one people because they happened to share a heritage. That heritage was not only Mexican; it was also Spanish-speaking. For the school boards, assumptions about language skills, cleanliness, ability to learn, and Americanness were code words for long-established anti–Latin American prejudices. *Mendez* exposed these to the light of social science and law and found them wanting.

There are heroes in this story: the parents themselves and, more quietly, their children; their counsel; a thoughtful federal district court judge; and those in the community who saw the injustice of discriminatory pupil placement. But Strum is scrupulously fair to the superintendents, school board heads, principals, and their counsel who argued for the segregation of the Mexican-American students—fair in the sense that she allows them to speak for themselves, to make their best case.

Indeed, one of the many strengths of this book is Strum's ability to take readers back to the time and place of the litigation and allow them to listen as the parties speak their piece. Weaving together the court records, contemporary accounts, later oral histories, and other scholars' work, she enables us to hear all the voices of the protagonists, and we find ourselves eagerly following the story toward its uplifting conclusion. Clearly, this is one case the courts got right.

ACKNOWLEDGMENTS

Writing is a solitary act, but getting all the information and feedback necessary to complete a work of nonfiction certainly is not. As always, I am indebted to a wide array of friends, colleagues, acquaintances, archivists, and librarians.

Friends first. Jill Norgren has vetted my manuscripts for years and did so again with *Mendez*, working her way meticulously through a very rough draft and making a slew of helpful suggestions. John Ferren, Michael Jones-Correa, and Peter Rajsingh each commented from the perspective of their particular areas of expertise. Susan Nugent did her usual painstaking read of the manuscript, catching errors of both style and substance. The members of the Red Line Group — Marie Therese Connolly, Mary Ellen Curtin, Matt Dallek, Deirdre Maloney, Robyn Muncy, Patricia Sullivan, Wendy Williams, and Salim Yaqub — weighed in with both fine critiques and unending support, and I dedicate this volume to them in happy anticipation of many more evenings of scholarly insights and good cheer.

Next, colleagues and acquaintances — and what a delightful corollary benefit it is to make new acquaintances in the course of writing a book. Judge Frederick Aguirre, who has written about *Mendez* himself, shared his thinking, pointed me in the direction of many other helpful people, and became my resident expert on Mexican-Americans in the military. Christopher Arriola, another *Mendez* author, chatted about the case, gave me access to his files, and sent me copies of newspaper articles and school board minutes. Charles Wollenberg generously read and commented on a draft. Vicki L. Ruiz sent me her own articles and helped me find both research assistants in California and people involved in the case. As he so frequently does, Don Wolfensberger, my colleague at the Woodrow Wilson International Center for Scholars, patiently tracked down important material that I could not seem to find for myself.

Sylvia Méndez not only shared her time and memories and documents but also chauffeured me around Fullerton, California. Karen Melissa Marcus, one of David Marcus's grandchildren, answered question after question and sent photographs of her grandparents. She put me in touch with Marcus's daughter Maria Lane and two other grandchildren, Stephen DeLapp and Anne McIntyre. Steven and Daniel W. Holden sent information about their father. I am grateful to all of them. Judge Robert Carter, who wrote the NAACP's brief in *Mendez*, graciously permitted me to put him through a long interview. Alex Maldonado was equally gracious during a lengthy telephone interview.

I corresponded with a number of scholars, each of whom gave me thoughts and bits of data that helped a topic come alive. Thanks, therefore, to Carlos Blanton, Ruben Flores, Michael Olivas, and Kathleen Weiler — none of whom should be held responsible for any errors I may have committed. I am grateful as well to all the other scholars whose fine works on Mexican-American history were so helpful. They are listed in the bibliographic essay.

Clara E. Rodriguez of Fordham University and Terry McCaffrey of the U.S. Postal Service helped me with the history of the commemorative *Mendez* stamp. Jane Zamarripa, an intern with the Latin American Program at the Wilson Center, translated articles in *La Opinión*. I am grateful to Christine Eubank and Giovanni Hortua Vargas, who winnowed out information from newspapers in California archives. Special thanks go to Ashley Bohrer, my Wilson Center research assistant par excellence, for her talents, enthusiasm, and patient persistence.

I owe thanks to many librarians and archivists, but none more so than Janet Spikes, the extraordinary librarian of the Woodrow Wilson International Center for Scholars, who manages to find sources that have eluded others for years. Her staff, Dagne Gizaw and Michelle Kamalich, were endlessly helpful. My gratitude to the many people who dug through files and sent crucial information and documents: Michael Hironymous at the University of Texas at Austin's Benson Latin American Collection; Randy Thompson, National Archives and Records Administration–Pacific Region in Laguna Niguel, California; Charles Miller, National Archives and Records Administration–Pacific Region in San Bruno, California; Mora Prestinary, Orange County Public Library; John Elliott, Santa Ana History Room; Chris Jepsen of the Orange County Archives; and Jack W. Golden, senior assistant county counsel of Orange County.

I am grateful as always for the continuing support of the particularly nice and talented people at the University Press of Kansas, especially editor in chief Michael Briggs and assistant director and marketing manager Susan Schott. Thanks as well to Larisa Martin for overseeing the production process and to Karl Janssen for designing the striking cover.

Above all, I must thank the Woodrow Wilson International Center for Scholars, which has blessed me with space in which to work, research assistance, library privileges, an information technology staff able to tame my sometimes recalcitrant computer, and a host of colleagues with whom to trade ideas during working sessions and indulge in far less cerebral conversation in moments of relaxation. The Center is sheer bliss for scholars, and I am fortunate to be part of it.

Introduction

Soledad Vidaurri walked up to the schoolhouse door, five little children in her wake. It was a warm September 1943 day in Westminster, California, home to some 2,500 residents and right in the heart of citrus-growing country. American soldiers were still fighting overseas — almost two more years of battles lay ahead before World War II would end — but Orange County was peaceful and bustling economically because of the wartime demand for agricultural products and war factory materiel. Mrs. Vidaurri had come to the Westminster Main School to enroll her two daughters — Alice and Virginia Vidaurri — and her niece and two nephews — Sylvia Méndez, Gonzalo Méndez Jr., and Jerome Méndez — in the neighborhood public school.

Notice the last names. They're important.

Mrs. Vidaurri was welcomed to the school and was told that her daughters could be registered. Their father had a French ancestor, and their last name sounded acceptably French or Belgian to the teacher in charge of admissions. Besides, the Vidaurri girls were light-skinned. The Méndez children, however, were visibly darker and, to the teacher, their last name was all too clearly Mexican. They would have to be taken to the "Mexican" school a few blocks away. Little Gonzalo Jr. would remember the teacher telling his aunt, " 'We'll take those,' " indicating the two Vidaurri girls, " 'but we won't take those three.' " "We were too dark," Gonzalo recalled.

"No way," an outraged Mrs. Vidaurri replied, and marched all the children home. Her equally outraged brother, Gonzalo Méndez, simply refused to send his children to the "Mexican" school. Two years later the Méndezes would lead a group of Mexican-American parents into federal court, challenging the segregation of their children, and legal history would be made.

What follows is a story about Mexican-Americans standing up for their rights and about the other Americans who helped make the fight successful. There were many courageous figures in the tale of *Mendez v. Westminster* — Soledad Vidaurri certainly qualifies — but this is a relatively short book, so it focuses only on three men and one woman. One of the men is Gonzalo Méndez, father of the three Méndez children; the woman is their mother, Felícitas Méndez. The second man is David Marcus, a Jewish attorney, and the third is an Irish-American Catholic judge named Paul McCormick.

The other heroes and heroines of the tale are Mexican-American parents living in Southern California in the 1940s. The four who joined Gonzalo Méndez in bringing the 1946 school desegregation case, and the others who helped with moral and financial support, were not thinking in terms of heroism; they simply wanted their children to get the best possible education. The suit they filed claimed that the arbitrary placement of the children in Orange County's segregated "Mexican" public schools violated their constitutional right to an equal education. The effort behind the case involved many members of the local Mexican-American community, and the outcome energized Mexican-Americans fighting for equality throughout California and elsewhere in the Southwest.

For Mexican-Americans, the decision in *Mendez* was as important as the 1954 case of *Brown v. Board of Education*, in which the U.S. Supreme Court held that segregated schools for African-American children were unconstitutional. *Mendez*, in fact, had a direct impact on the attorneys of the National Association for the Advancement of Colored People (NAACP) who would later take *Brown* all the way to the Supreme Court. It also displayed the arbitrary nature of racial categories and the complicated relationship between what is happening in American society at any given moment and what is happening in American law. *Mendez* is, in many ways, the story of how and why law evolves, as well as the saga of all the people who made *Mendez* a landmark in American history and law.

The tale of what these people accomplished begins on land owned by Japanese-Americans and leased by Mexican-Americans. As it unfolds, the nation's largest African-American civil rights organization becomes involved, and so do associations of Jewish-Americans and Japanese-Americans. It is not a melting pot story, but more like a kaleidoscope.

{ *Introduction* }

In telling the tale of *Mendez*, I use Méndez (with the accent) when speaking about members of the Méndez family. I refer to the case as *Mendez* (without the accent) because the court personnel who transcribed the trial proceedings and prepared the judicial opinions for publication omitted it. The same is true for all Hispanic names in other court cases mentioned here.

The word *Mexican* was used throughout the litigation to describe children of Mexican descent, whether American citizens or not, and although it sometimes seemed appropriate to follow that usage in the narrative that follows, for the most part, I use *Mexican-American*. (I do not use *Chicano*, as that expression was not common in the 1940s.) Other children were referred to as *Anglo* or *Anglo-Saxon* or *white*. For the sake of convenience, I sometimes employ these terms where they make the context clear. As we will see, however, one of the issues in the case was whether *white* was appropriately differentiated from *Mexican* or *Latin*.

CHAPTER I

Mexican-Americans in California

A minority is somebody everyone else thinks is different and worse.
MEXICAN-AMERICAN SCHOOLBOY, 1940S

Mexicans had lived in California for hundreds of years before Gonzalo and Felícitas Méndez went to court in 1945. Or, rather, for much of that time they had lived in a part of Mexico, known as California, that would be absorbed by the United States. In 1846 the United States' desire to annex Texas plunged it and Mexico into the Mexican-American War. The conflict ended with the 1848 Treaty of Guadalupe Hidalgo, which forced Mexico to cede a large part of its territory. All of what would become the states of California, Arizona, and New Mexico, as well as Texas and parts of what would become Colorado, Nevada, and Utah, were folded into the United States. The treaty gave resident Mexicans the option of returning to Mexico or declaring themselves permanent resident aliens in the United States. If they chose neither option within one year, they would become American citizens with, according to the treaty, "all the rights of citizens." These new citizens and their descendants were commonly referred to by others as *Californios*.

Other Mexicans immigrated to the United States in the decades after the war. By 1900, the American Mexican population had increased from 116,000 to an estimated 500,000 out of a total of 76,212,168 people living in the United States. Their migration, as is the case with many waves of immigration, reflected both a "push" from the home country and a "pull" by the receiving country.

The push was the economic and political turmoil that occurred in Mexico beginning in 1876, when Porfirio Díaz became the country's president. His administration sought to better Mexico's economy by encouraging foreign investment, the commercialization of agriculture, and the fashioning of large *haciendas* (ranches or farms) capable of producing exportable crops. The haciendas were created by seizing what had been communal lands, and as many as 5 million Mexicans soon found themselves landless. Simultaneously, the emphasis on producing crops for export led to a decrease in the production of maize, which was the key food staple for most families. The price of food went up; the cost of living in general rose; and at the same time, the labor surplus created by the Díaz land policy resulted in a decline of wages.

The Mexican Revolution, which began in 1910, was in large part a reaction to the Díaz regime. For the next ten years civil war roiled Mexico, and hundreds of thousands died. Many Mexicans were by then looking for an escape and a more promising life — Gonzalo Méndez's family was among them — and thousands believed that the new network of Mexican railroads going north would lead them to it.

Railroads in the United States had grown as well, expanding into the American West in the decades after the end of the American Civil War. Simultaneously, advances in irrigation enabled western growers to produce large quantities of fruits and vegetables, which could be transported in the newly invented refrigerator cars on the railroads that now crisscrossed the United States. That became the pull for Mexican immigrants, as the need for cheap labor among both the growers and the railroads increased exponentially. Mexicans would replace Chinese and Japanese as farmhands and layers of railroad tracks.

The railroads and farms had encouraged the immigration of Chinese laborers to California in the 1850s and 1860s. Prejudice and the concerns of native American workers about a competitive labor force, however, caused Congress to enact the Chinese Exclusion Act of 1882, effectively minimizing the number of Chinese who could gain entry to the United States. Agricultural and railroad corporations then turned to Japanese immigrants, but farm owners soon found that the Japanese were too well organized for their purposes. The immigrants banded together to demand better working conditions and refused to compete with one another; they organized to become highly competitive entrepreneurs themselves. The growers' resentment of the Japanese farmers' assertiveness, coupled with the racism that seemed endemic to the country, resulted in the so-called Gentlemen's Agreement of 1907 between the United States and Japan. It took the form of a pact between President Theodore Roosevelt and the Japanese government and gave the president the power to refuse entry to Japanese would-be immigrants — a power Roosevelt used vigorously.

The agribusinesses then turned to Mexicans as a labor supply. They were not interested in recruiting new citizens; rather, they were determined to maintain a cheap labor supply, and their disdain for their workers was obvious in the way they treated the new arrivals. Mexican workers who remained in the United States permanently would face the same kind of contempt and discrimination that had been meted out to the Chinese and Japanese.

They were nonetheless viewed by Anglo employers as necessary. Nativist fears about the immigrants flooding into the eastern United States from Europe led Congress to enact a country-by-country immigration quota in 1921 and again in 1924. Owing to pressure from the western growers, now dependent on Mexican labor, the countries of the Western Hemisphere were exempt from the quotas. The result was that Mexicans, along with any other immigrants who could make their way to the United States from Central and South America, constituted the only large-scale source of potential new workers. They were particularly welcomed by growers during World War I, when many American workers were sent off to fight in Europe and others moved from farms into war industries. Labor agents recruited workers in Mexico and arranged transportation to the United States for them.

The numbers were impressive. By the mid-1920s, Mexican workers constituted the bulk of farm laborers throughout the citrus groves of Southern California (the area where Gonzalo Méndez would bring his case to court) and accounted for three-quarters of all California farmworkers. In 1930 the U.S. Chamber of Commerce stated that Mexicans picked more than 80 percent of the Southwest's crops. Official census figures indicated that 661,538 Mexicans entered the United States between 1910 and 1930. Scholars question that number, however. Historian David Gutiérrez estimates that between 1 million and 1.5 million Mexicans migrated to the United States between 1890 and 1929. Vicki Ruiz, another historian, puts the figure at more than 1 million between 1910 and 1930 alone, thereby suggesting that one-eighth to one-tenth of the entire Mexican population moved north. The disparity between the scholars' calculations and the official numbers reflects the difficulty of getting into the United States, which led many Mexicans to enter the country illegally.

They were given every incentive to do so by the way they were treated at the border. During World War I, American customs agents sprayed Mexicans coming across the Santa Fe bridge in Texas, the main entry point at the border, with insecticides, gasoline, kerosene, and cyanide-based pesticides. The immigrants were forced to strip off their clothing, which, along with their baggage, was fumigated and deloused, while they were made to go through a public bath. Like all immigrants to the United States after 1917, they had to pay a head tax and a visa fee; those older than sixteen also had to take a literacy test (given in Spanish at the Mexican border crossing points). It was largely young men who had made the trek from Mexico to the workplaces of the Southwest in the late nineteenth century, returning home to their families when they had saved some money and then making the round-trip again and again. The horrors of the border crossing in the early decades of the twentieth century, however, discouraged immigrants from such circular migration. Whole families came to the United States or arrived one or a few at a time, sending for other family members later. As a result, permanent concentrations of Mexican families—wanted for their labor, but not considered part of the "real" United States—were established throughout the Southwest. Corporate farms may have welcomed the workers, but the American suspicion of immigrants would not make the welcome an easy one.

The Mexicans arrived in a country with a long history of skepticism about immigrants. The United States is, of course, a nation of immigrants, but almost every new group making the journey has been greeted with hostility by members of groups that arrived earlier. Irish, Italian, and Jewish immigrants, for example, found no warm welcome in the nineteenth and early twentieth centuries. Irish immigrants faced job discrimination; some hotels bore signs proclaiming, "No Dogs or Jews"; Sicilian immigrants were lynched in Colorado and Illinois as well as in Louisiana and other southern states. Ethnic groups ate their own foods, and they usually ate them at home. In the first decades of the twentieth century, when many Mexican immigrants crossed the border, the local Chinese restaurant and the neighborhood pizza parlor simply did not exist. A town with a Thai restaurant or a taco parlor at the strip mall was inconceivable, and not only because strip malls did not yet exist. The United States was still a largely rural nation. Most Americans knew nothing about other ethnic and religious groups and, having almost no opportunity to meet them, regarded them with suspicion. There was no *Sesame Street* to teach children multiculturalism; in fact, American homes did not begin to acquire television sets in significant numbers until well after World War II.

The suspicion of immigrants was exacerbated by the fact that most of them, including those from Mexico, journeyed to the United States out of economic necessity — that is, they were poor. Because the United States was built on the assumption that anyone who worked hard could succeed and anyone who had not succeeded probably did not deserve to do so, Americans tended to look down on poor people. So the Mexicans who arrived at border crossing points encountered immigration officials whose less-than-welcoming attitudes reflected the values of the country they represented.

There were some middle-class Mexicans crossing the border, primarily for political rather than economic reasons, and they were frequently spared the indignities inflicted by border officials on those who were more poorly dressed or not as well-spoken. The young woman who would later marry Gonzalo and Felícitas Méndez's lawyer was among them. Most of the immigrants, however, had little money. Many of them settled in poorer neighborhoods — *colonias* — next to citrus groves or vegetable fields, on the outskirts of cities such as Santa Ana, California. Santa Ana is the county seat of Orange County, where the Méndez story takes place. It and the rest of the citrus belt were particularly conducive to permanent settlement because employment was to be had there for most of the year. Navel oranges had a long winter-to-spring picking season; Valencia oranges had a different and equally long summer–to–early winter season. Although oranges and lemons were the big crops, the farms also grew nuts, beans, and vegetables. Families might move to other parts of California from time to time to pick other crops, but they would return home for the long citrus seasons.

The Mexican farm laborers who lived on the outskirts of Anglo towns in Orange County in the 1930s found themselves in neighborhoods that for the most part lacked sewers, gas for cooking and heating, paved streets, or sidewalks. Many families built their own two-room wooden houses and could afford very little furniture. There were no refrigerators; heat came from wood-burning kitchen stoves. Clothes were made on pedal-powered sewing machines and cleaned in washtubs. The families might have small food gardens and raise chickens, goats, or ducks. With dirt streets, a lack of flush toilets, and inadequate plumbing and heating, it was difficult to maintain good sanitation. Tuberculosis was a constant threat and affected the Mexican-American community at a rate three to five times that of the Anglo community. A survey undertaken in the late 1920s found that the average Mexican couple had buried two children, and many had buried three or more.

Half the men in the *colonias* surveyed had been unemployed for 100 or more working days in 1927; 73 percent were unemployed for 60 or more working days. When they did work, the average wage for men was 38 cents an hour; for women, whether they worked in the fields or in packinghouses, it was 27 cents. (The average wage for all male workers in the United States that year was 61 cents; for women, 40 cents.) Their wages, in other words, could not provide adequate food, shelter, and clothing. There was no sick pay, no payment for injuries sustained on the job, no guarantee that even an underpaid job would be waiting for someone who had to stop working temporarily. The permanent existence of a largely disenfranchised laboring class has been described by Christopher Arriola as a "citrus society," similar to the exploitative "cotton society" that flourished in the South in the late nineteenth century. In both instances, the land was owned primarily by Anglos and worked by discriminated-against minority group members.

There was, however, a strong sense of community. The workers and their families established *mutualistas* — mutual aid societies — along with church societies, patriotic associations, sports teams, and entertainment groups. In some instances the *mutualistas* provided a modicum of unemployment and medical insurance to their members, along with funds for labor organizing and money to pay for funerals. The communities were poor, but they were both dynamic and cohesive.

Fear of the "other" that the communities and their inhabitants generated among non-Mexican Americans and fear of competition for jobs resulted in the U.S. Census Bureau announcing in 1930 that it considered "Mexican" to denote a separate race. Mexicans, it declared, were people who were born in Mexico or in the United States to Mexican parents and who were not "definitely white, Negro, Indian [Native American], Chinese, or Japanese." The Mexican government was outraged — Mexicans living in the United States considered themselves white — and, faced with pressure from an American administration concerned about international relations, the Census Bureau agreed to drop the category. The 1940 census reclassified Mexicans as white if they were not "definitely Indian or of other nonwhite race." As they had been before, Mexicans were officially not black, nor were they "Indians"; they were "white." In a society that created the phenomenon of racial categories and then judged people according to where they fit into them, the Mexicans could take whatever comfort they might choose in their classification as part of the dominant race.

It came as something of a shock, then, when community life was threatened by one aspect of Americans' reaction to the Depression that began in 1929. The Depression put one-quarter of the country's workers, almost 12.5 million of them, out of jobs. Looking for a scapegoat, labor unions and newly unemployed Americans charged that Mexicans and other illegal immigrants were taking bread out of their families' mouths. Many non-Mexican Americans believed that all Mexicans in the United States were migrant workers who had entered the country illegally, rather than, as was by then the case for most, American citizens or the parents of American citizens living in established communities. The workers' status as "white" did not protect them. In 1931 President Herbert Hoover and Secretary of Labor William N. Doak responded to popular fervor by authorizing a drive to deport "aliens," which in fact resulted in the departure of many Mexican-American citizens. In California, which had begun deportation efforts a few years earlier, Los Angeles County and other counties identified Mexican families on welfare rolls and threatened them with deportation unless they left voluntarily. The deportations were widely publicized by local English and Spanish newspapers, frightening Mexicans and Mexican-American citizens alike into believing that if they left voluntarily they might be permitted to return. Between 1929 and 1932, more than 365,000 Mexicans and Mexican-Americans were repatriated to Mexico. An estimated one-third of the entire American Mexican population, comprising more than 500,000 people, left voluntarily or otherwise, even though perhaps 60 percent of them were American citizens. In 1930 at least 2,000 "Mexicans" were repatriated from Orange County alone.

Faced with prejudice and the realization that their position in the United States was far from secure, some American Mexicans fought

10   { *Chapter 1* }

back. This was particularly true in the field of labor organizing. Mexican workers in the United States organized strikes and picket lines, some of them in coordination with the American Federation of Labor, at least as early as the first decades of the twentieth century. In 1927 Mexican laborers created the Confederación de Uniones Obreras Mexicanas (Confederation of Mexican Workers' Unions, or CUOM), which would soon number 3,000 workers in twenty Southern California locals. CUOM organized its first strike in the Imperial Valley, near Orange County, in 1928. Although that strike was broken by the growers, a second one in 1930 was successful, and the growers were forced to settle with the union. There were more than sixteen major strikes in California between 1933 and 1937, some of them organized by another labor association, the Confederación de Uniones de Campesinos y Obreros Mexicanos. The growers frequently reacted violently. The unsuccessful strike of 1936 was particularly violent, as growers, local law enforcement officers, special deputies, and the California Highway Patrol combined to beat strikers and force them back to work. Women were prominent in the strike, leading the *Orange Daily News* to print a banner headline proclaiming, "Women Join Strike . . . Women Stage Citrus Riots at Anaheim," followed by a story deploring the involvement of "two hundred angry Mexican women, described as 'Amazons' with the fire of battle in their eyes." Mexicans and Mexican-Americans were far from passive victims, although the concessions they were able to wrest from the growers were insufficient to guarantee a decent standard of living.

Workers' rights were also the concern of El Congreso de Pueblos de Habla Española (Congress of Spanish-Speaking Peoples), which held its first congress in Los Angeles in 1939. Nearly 1,000 delegates from 128 Latino-oriented organizations in the United States and Mexico attended. The congress, which owed much of its success to two Latinas — Luisa Moreno and Josefina Fierro de Bright — emphasized education, housing, health, and desegregation, and it also urged equality for women.

The importance of these efforts to the Méndez story lies in their helping to create a tradition of fighting back against perceived discrimination and injustice. It did not involve the majority of Mexican-Americans, but it was a tradition that could be drawn upon when the moment was right.

Mexican-Americans organized outside the field of labor as well. Many of those who fought for the United States in World War I returned determined to fight equally hard against discrimination at home. In Texas they found allies in a small but burgeoning Mexican-American middle class — attorneys, teachers, small entrepreneurs — and by 1921 they had formed a number of organizations. Some of the groups came together in 1929, creating the League of United Latin American Citizens (LULAC).

The emphasis was on the last three words in the organization's name: "Latin American Citizens." Only citizens of the United States could join LULAC, which conducted all its activities in English. Latin American citizens were full citizens, LULAC proclaimed proudly, entitled to all the rights and privileges of other Americans, and LULAC was prepared to use all legal means to ensure those rights. Unlike the *mutualistas*, LULAC did not seek to provide social services. Its organizers announced that LULAC would focus on the rights of Mexican-Americans to vote; serve on juries; have full access to public facilities such as restaurants, movie theaters, swimming pools, and barbershops; buy and rent housing in all neighborhoods; and attend desegregated schools. Each of these areas reflected the pervasiveness of discrimination. Mexican-Americans were unwelcome in white neighborhoods and in places of public accommodation, and they were rarely selected for jury service. They were also shunted to inferior schools — a story that is detailed in the following pages. LULAC's constitution proclaimed that the organization hoped "to assume complete responsibility for the education of our children as to their rights and duties and the language and customs of this country." The assumption was that access to equal educational opportunity was a first step and that economic and social assimilation would follow quickly. By 1939, LULAC had about 2,000 members, with chapters throughout the Southwest; by the early 1940s, it had at least eighty chapters in New Mexico, Arizona, California, and Kansas, as well as in Texas.

Nonetheless, the LULAC of the 1930s and 1940s was an underfunded if growing entity that lacked a large professional staff. It could not afford to fight for school desegregation by bringing costly legal cases, so it employed pressure group tactics instead: negotiations with school boards and other elected officials in some instances, threats of boycotts in others. Most of these activities took place in Texas and achieved some, but limited, success.

In one instance, however, LULAC did bring a school desegregation case. To understand why, it is necessary to examine the state of Mexican-American public school education in the years that preceded *Mendez v. Westminster*.

The history of public school education in California, which is not substantially different from that in Texas and the other southwestern states, is a story of racism colliding with the government's obligation to provide for the schooling of all children. In 1855, seven years after the Treaty of Guadalupe Hidalgo was signed, California enacted a law requiring the State School Fund to "be apportioned to counties on the basis of a census of white children, ages 4 to 18." That was followed, in 1860, by another state law prohibiting "colored children" from attending integrated schools but permitting school districts to operate separate schools, if they chose to do so, for blacks, Indians, and Asians. Education, in short, was crucial for children labeled "white" but not for others. The question of the education of those other children remained, however, and in 1866, California ordered every school district to establish a separate school for black children if at least ten black parents formally requested it. In the 1870s, African-American and Indian children were allowed to attend white schools only where no other schools were available, and in 1874 the California Supreme Court specifically endorsed the segregation of African-American children in separate schools (*Ward v. Flood*). That year the California legislature mandated compulsory school attendance for all children aged eight through fourteen, and in 1880 it decreed that schools had to admit all children except for "children of filthy or vicious habits, or children suffering from contagious or infectious diseases." Nonetheless, Chinese children were for the most part not permitted in public schools at all (San Francisco was the exception) until they were given that right by an 1885 court case (*Tape v. Hurley*), after which many communities established separate Chinese schools.

Most Californians were still not prepared to see children of different races sitting in school together. A nineteenth-century California law specifically gave school districts the authority to create separate schools for "Indian children, excepting children of Indians who are wards of the United States government and children of all other Indians who are descendants of the original American Indians of the United States, and for children of Chinese, Japanese or Mongolian parentage." Mexican children were not mentioned, presumably because there were still relatively few of them and because the children of the relatively wealthy *Californios* were considered socially acceptable. That omission became controversial as Mexicans migrated to the United States in the 1920s. In 1929, asked for legal advice, the California attorney general issued an advisory opinion stating that Mexican children were not covered by the law and so separate schools should not be organized for them. Two years later, California assemblyman George R. Bliss introduced a bill that would have expanded the clause about Indian children to enable the segregation of "Indian children whether born in the United States or not." The purpose was to permit districts to segregate Mexican and Mexican-American children, who were perceived by Bliss and his allies as Indian. The bill was defeated, but its intent was made clear by a supporter who spoke of "slip[ping] the bill through the state legislature so we can segregate these greasers." The school segregation law, amended slightly in 1935, became a crucial element in the *Mendez* case.

Continuing immigration from Mexico, along with a high birthrate for Mexicans in California, meant that by the early decades of the twentieth century, there were more and more Mexican and Mexican-American children to be schooled. By 1927 such children, 64,427 of them, constituted nearly 10 percent of all children enrolled in California's public schools, and the 2,869 who were enrolled in Orange County made up 17 percent of that county's public school population. In nearby Imperial County they totaled more than 26 percent. By the mid-1920s, El Modena, which was one of the four towns involved in *Mendez v. Westminster*, had 1,000 Mexican and Mexican-American residents, who made up a majority of the town's population.

Many of the families were dependent on the children laboring in the fields alongside their parents for part of the school day. Some moved their children out of the local school districts during the months when the families followed the crops to other areas. Many of the children entered school speaking only Spanish. Given the

14   *{ Chapter 1 }*

appalling sanitary conditions in which too many of the families were forced to live, it is not surprising that some children arrived at school each day unbathed. The school authorities worried about the spread of diseases such as tuberculosis. The attendance and health problems were real, but as *Mendez* would indicate, the way the children were treated had as much to do with racism as with concern for their well-being. The solution preferred by the school districts became permanent educational segregation.

Pasadena therefore established a "Mexican" school in 1913, and all children identified as such were required to attend it. La Habra opened a similar school in 1920, making certain that it included showers so that the children could satisfy the teachers' notions of cleanliness before they began their lessons. Ontario followed suit with a "Mexican" school in 1921 and another in 1928. Orange County joined the trend. By the mid-1920s, there were fifteen such schools in Orange County, all but one located in the citrus-growing areas that would be involved in *Mendez v. Westminster*. According to one survey, by 1931, more than 80 percent of all California school districts with a significant number of Mexican (non–American citizen) and Mexican-American students were segregated, usually through the careful drawing of school zone boundaries by school boards that had been pressured by Anglo residents. The ostensible rationale for the separate schools was the children's lack of proficiency in English.

Santa Ana initially took another route, setting aside a special room for "Spanish" elementary school children as early as 1913. The students were taught a curriculum quite different from the one offered to non-"Spanish" children. The "Spanish" boys studied gardening, bootmaking, blacksmithing, and carpentry to prepare them for the low-paying trades that school authorities assumed would be the only ones such boys could or should follow. The girls studied sewing and homemaking. In 1916, Santa Ana's Committee on Buildings decided to build a wholly separate school for the children, with a curriculum similarly different from the white curriculum and with different criteria for the selection of teachers. According to the district superintendent, "This school will make it possible to give such children" (referring to those "who are unable to speak or understand the English language") "personal attention and a kind of training suited to their needs."

When the building was completed and it was time for the children to be moved, their parents objected strenuously. The Pro Patria Club of Santa Ana demanded that the children remain enrolled in the newly "white" school. The Santa Ana school board consulted the city attorney, who agreed that the board had no authority to place the children in separate schools based on race but, as recorded in the school board's minutes, determined that "it is entirely proper and legal to classify them according to the regularity of attendance, ability to understand the English language and their aptness to advance in the grades to which they shall be assigned." The "aptness" of Mexican-American students "to advance in the grades to which they shall be assigned" became a key point in *Mendez*. In 1919, however, the parents' protest was to no avail, and the children were moved to the new school.

The following year the Santa Ana school board divided the town into fourteen elementary school zones, drawn to create three "Mexican" schools. "White" families living in those three zones were permitted to transfer their children to other schools. The teachers at the Mexican schools earned $960 a year; those at the Anglo schools, $1,040. Principals at the "Mexican" schools earned $135 less per year than their counterparts at "white" schools.

Some years later, in 1928, two University of Southern California professors were asked by the Santa Ana school district to conduct a survey of all its schools. The professors found that Delhi, one of the "Mexican" schools, was a wooden fire hazard. They reported that another, the Artesia School, "has a low single roof with no air space, which makes the temperature in many of the rooms almost unbearable. Since no artificial light is provided in the building, it is impossible to do satisfactory reading without serious eye strain on many days of the year." The board decided to ignore concerns about the first school but to build a new Artesia School, which opened in the 1929–1930 school year and was renamed the Fremont School. It would figure prominently in *Mendez*.

The hazardous Delhi School was not atypical among Orange County's "Mexican" schools, which were usually built of wood, while the "white" schools were made out of brick or block masonry. Shower stalls were common in the "Mexican" schools, and children whom the teachers considered dirty were required to take showers and, if necessary, borrow clean clothing from a cupboard kept for that purpose.

Books and other equipment were castoffs from the "white" schools. One former El Modena student interviewed by Christopher Arriola recalled the difference between the curriculum at the "white" Roosevelt School and that at the "Mexican" Lincoln School: "I remember math, . . . a little bit of biology, science, we'd never really heard of that at Lincoln and I know they were being taught stuff like that at Roosevelt." Many of the "Mexican" schools opened at 7:30 in the morning and ended the day at 12:30, so the children could go to work in the citrus groves. Even so, although 95 percent of eligible students were enrolled in the schools, attendance was less than perfect. As mentioned earlier, families frequently moved to other areas during the picking seasons for walnuts and various other fruits and vegetables, taking their children with them. Not surprisingly, many students had to repeat grades, and they dropped out of school as soon as they could.

In the late 1920s an Anglo researcher undertook a survey of schools in San Bernardino County, northeast of Orange County. The investigator, a leading California educator named Merton Earle Hill, was particularly concerned about the "over-ageness" and "retardation" of what he called "Mexican" children, even though he acknowledged that a large majority of them had been born in the United States and were therefore American citizens. "Over-ageness" and "retardation" referred to children being held back in school while others of their age were promoted to the next grades. "The average thirteen, fourteen, and fifteen-year-old children . . . who are children of Mexican peon parents," Hill wrote, "are normally four years behind the children of normal American parentage. As soon as the compulsory education law ceases to control the attendance, the children of Mexican peon parents drop out." Hill defined "Mexican peon" as "the type of Mexican who is a worker" and is "descended either from the native Indians of Mexico, or from the native Indian stock mixed with a Spanish, or even with a Negro strain."

Hill recited figures about wages and living conditions, indicating that the children had made the lamentable error of being born into poverty, and commented that "children living under such conditions could not progress as well in school even if they possessed as much native ability as the normal American children" — which, Hill determined, they did not. Hill's testing of the students led him to conclude that Mexicans and "Negro" students had 67.5 percent of the Americans' abilities. Mexicans had only 58.1 percent of the other students' ability to pursue academic courses.

Their one redeeming grace was that they had "90 percent as good ability as have American pupils to do manual work." Hill's strong recommendation, therefore, was that Mexican students be given a separate course of study. They would be immersed in an "Americanization" program that would include English, "simple arithmetic lessons leading to a mastery of the four fundamental processes," and an emphasis on penmanship, "for they appear to be adept in a certain manual dexterity that leads to proficiency in penmanship." Asserting that "Mexicans are lovers of music and art" and so should be given lessons in those subjects, Hill continued, "As the Mexicans show considerable aptitude for hand work of any kind courses should be developed that will aid them in becoming skilled workers with their hands. Girls should be trained to become domestic servants, and to do various kinds of hand work for which they can be paid adequately after they leave school." Boys should be taught "to make inexpensive furniture for the home — to make use of discarded tin cans in the development of useful kitchen utensils. . . . Girls should be trained to become neat and efficient house servants." Having set out a program for the production of low-paid workers, Hill added that these future workers should be taught thrift as well, because "it is a well known fact . . . that the Mexican laborers are not possessed of thrift." He did not address the question of how families with wages of 38 cents an hour survived without practicing thrift.

"Americanization" programs such as those advocated by Hill became a statewide goal in California in 1916, when the Division of Immigrant Education was established within the state's Department of Education to develop and promote them. Santa Ana quickly established a similar program of its own. A year earlier, the California Home Teaching Act had empowered school districts to send teachers into Mexican-American schools, instructing both children and adults about attendance, sanitation, English, "household duties," and "the fundamental principles of the American system of government and the rights and duties of citizenship." The program expanded after World War I, but in the late 1920s the educators shifted their focus to separating Mexican-American children from their parents' culture.

As historian Gilbert G. González has noted, "Teachers urged Mexican children to 'make fun of the lazy ones' in the classroom; to overcome uncleanliness by making a dirty child feel uncomfortable," and "to compare Mexican and American homes for the sake of imitation."

Hill himself had the chance to put his theories into action: he was the superintendent of the Ontario, California, school system. His study earned him a doctorate in education from the Graduate Division of the University of California in 1928 and became extremely influential. It reflected and affected an attitude of educators toward Mexican-American students that was supposedly based on scientific principles. The function of the public schools was to integrate children into what the educators regarded as the American way of life — a way of life that emphasized work, cleanliness, manners, and a scorn for anything as "un-American" as the Spanish language or Mexican culture. As Mexican-American children were perceived as coming to school without the benefits of socialization into the American ethos, they were best off being educated separately from other students. They were happiest in segregated schools, where they could thrive with other unfortunates just like themselves, California educator Grace Stanley asserted in an influential 1920 article entitled "Special School for Mexicans." She added that Mexican children had "different mental characteristics" than Anglo children, "showed a stronger sense of rhythm," and "are primarily interested in action and emotion but grow listless under purely mental effort." Others echoed this assessment. B. F. Haught's 1931 study convinced him that the "average Spanish child has an intelligence quotient of .79 compared with 1.00 for the average Anglo child." William Sheldon, who gave IQ tests to Mexican and Anglo students in Texas, concluded that Mexicans had only 85 percent of the IQ of Anglos. A professor in Denver declared that the "Mexican" children's median IQ was a low 78.1. The academic pundits agreed that students should be encouraged to give up Spanish and develop their talents in industrial and vocational subjects. Emory Bogardus, a University of Southern California sociologist, urged that Mexican children be segregated so they would not have to suffer "invidious comparisons with Anglo students."

School boards throughout the state operated on the assumption that segregating what were viewed as the underachieving Mexican-American students was a good thing. By 1934, more than 4,000 pupils in Orange County — 25 percent of the county's total student enrollment — were Mexican or Mexican-American. Seventy percent of the county's students with Spanish surnames were registered in the fifteen Orange County elementary schools that had 100 percent Mexican enrollment. Six of the fifteen schools were in the four districts at issue in the *Mendez* case: three in Santa Ana and one each in Westminster, El Modena, and Garden Grove. Forty percent of the county's Mexican students lived in these four districts. Unlike the elementary schools, the high schools in rural Southern California were, for the most part, integrated. Rural districts could not afford more than one high school, but in any case, there were not enough Mexican-American students to warrant a separate high school. Many Mexican-Americans, repeatedly held back as "retarded," were still in the eighth grade when they turned sixteen years old and were able to drop out of school. Isabel Martínez graduated from Fullerton High School, in another Orange County citrus belt town, in 1931. That was so unusual — in fact, she was the first Mexican-American ever to graduate from Fullerton High — that the event was covered by the local newspaper. Sadly, there were few such graduates in subsequent years, in part because Mexican-Americans were not encouraged to complete high school and in part because there were so few appropriate job opportunities for Mexican-American graduates.

Alex Maldonado's experience with elementary school in the early 1930s was similar to that of many other Mexican-American children. The Maldonados lived on an Orange County farm. The children in the family walked half a mile every school day, rain or shine, to reach the place where the school bus picked them up. They then rode the three miles or so to Westminster. The bus dropped all the other children off at the Westminster Main School, to which the Méndezes would later try to send their children. The Maldonados, the only Latino children on the bus, also got off there and walked the three blocks to the segregated Westminster Hoover School. They had to walk because the bus driver declined to drive into the barrio, where Hoover was located. At some point, school authorities decided the children were in a different district, and they were transferred to the Hoover School in Garden Grove. They liked that a lot better because the Garden Grove school bus picked them up right in front of the farm. Then it picked up the Anglo children and drove into Garden

Grove, going right past the Hoover School to deliver the Anglo children to their school first, before taking the Latino students back to Hoover. The bus reversed the process at the end of the school day, collecting the Hoover children first and then picking up the Anglo ones. The Latino children had the longer ride in both directions, but that was of no concern to school authorities. When the Méndezes decided to attack school segregation some years later, Maldonado would be ready to help.

In the 1930s and 1940s there was a connection between attitudes about race and those toward class. There was, at the same time, a disconnect between legal status and social realities. Mexican immigrants and Mexican-Americans, whatever their class, were formally entitled to equal treatment by the law. They were legally white. They were nonetheless assumed by Anglo-Americans to belong to a different race and the lowliest of classes, and for that reason they were viewed as the legitimate objects of unequal treatment by employers as well as local officials.

At the same time, segregation was not total. In the rare instances in which Mexican-American families, most of them descendants of the original *Californios*, were relatively prosperous, their children were permitted to attend "white" schools. The fact that they performed well there did not seem to affect Anglo educators' assumptions about the intellectual failings of Mexican-Americans as a distinct and inferior race.

CHAPTER 2

From Lemon Grove to the Zoot Suit Riots

Mexican-American families did not simply accept their children's seg-regation, as the Pro Patria Club's protests in Santa Ana indicated, although there was little they could do. The parents were busy eking out their livelihoods, they had little or no access to the political sys-tem, and they were frequently hampered by a lack of fluency in En-glish. Nonetheless, in 1931, in a San Diego school district 100 miles south of Orange County, parents and their children revolted.

There were seventy-five Mexican-American students in the Lemon Grove Grammar School in 1930, the year the Lemon Grove school board, bowing to pressure from the Anglo-dominated Parent-Teacher Association and the local chamber of commerce, decided to build a separate school for them. When the school was ready to open on Jan-uary 5, 1931, the principal of the Lemon Grove Grammar School stood at its door and told the Mexican-American students they would have to go to the new building. Their desks and personal belongings had already been moved there. An idea of the wooden structure's amenities can be gathered from the nickname, La Caballeriza ("the stable"), that it was soon given by the community. Built squarely in the barrio, the school was furnished with secondhand books and supplies. Directed to their new school, the children simply returned home instead, and with the exception of only one family, their working-class parents refused to send them to it. The families formed El Comité de Veci-nos de Lemon Grove to fight the move and turned to the Mexican consul in San Diego for help. The consul promised financial help if the Comité could not raise adequate funds and put the parents in touch with two lawyers who had worked for the consulate. The fam-ilies decided to sue and asked the San Diego Superior Court (the local state trial court) to order the school board not to send the children to the new school. Student Roberto Álvarez, who was fluent in English, was chosen to be the lead plaintiff in the class-action suit—a suit brought on behalf of all people with the same interest—so the case became known as *Alvarez v. Lemon Grove School District*. It was at that point that Assemblyman Bliss introduced the bill that would have legitimized the segregation of Mexican "Indian" students.

The hearing, before Judge Claude Chambers, began on February 24, 1931. The San Diego district attorney told the court that the new school was needed because most of the students at issue began the school year late and could not speak English well, and added that the school had a really nice playground. The families' lawyers responded by calling a number of the children, most of whom had been born in the United States, to demonstrate their proficiency in English. In fact, one of the students spoke no Spanish whatsoever.

Judge Chambers, using the nomenclature "American" and "Mexican" that prevailed both in this case and in *Mendez*, asked a school official about the decision to segregate children on the basis of language deficiency:

> JUDGE CHAMBERS: When there are American children who are behind, what do you do with them?
> ANSWER: They are kept in a lower grade.
> JUDGE CHAMBERS: You don't segregate them? Why not do the same with the other children? Wouldn't the association of American and Mexican children be favorable to the learning of English for these children?
> ANSWER: [Silence].

The judge was unconvinced. "I understand that you can separate a few children, to improve their education they need special instruction," he said, "but to separate all the Mexicans in one group can only be done by infringing the laws of the State of California." State law, he reminded the school authorities, permitted the segregation of Asian children, but not Mexicans. In a statement that would be echoed in *Mendez*, he added, "I believe that this separation denies the Mexican children the presence of the American children, which is so necessary to learn the English language." (It was far too early in the United States' history for anyone to suggest that the American children might benefit from the presence of their Mexican peers.) He ordered the school board to permit the children back in their original school, and the board decided not to appeal. Because there was no appeal, the decision had no legal weight in any other district, and there is no indication that any other school district chose to heed Judge Chambers's words.

LULAC had filed a similar suit (*Salvatierra v. Del Rio Independent School District*) one year earlier in the Rio Grande border town of Del Rio, Texas. The Del Rio Independent School District sold a municipal bond that, in part, would enable it to add five rooms and an auditorium to the Mexican elementary school that housed grades one through three. The move made it clear to Mexican-American parents in Del Rio that the children in those grades would be segregated permanently, so they went to court. They did not argue a difference in facilities; rather, as *Mendez* would, they claimed that the segregation itself was illegal.

At trial, the school's superintendent justified the operation of a separate school in much the same way authorities in Lemon Grove had, citing poor attendance. The Mexican students would suffer from low self-esteem if they were held to the same standards as the children who had been in school from the beginning of the school year, he said, and their suffering would be increased by the embarrassment caused by their poor English language skills. The superintendent denied that "any motive of segregation by reason of race or color" was behind the move. His testimony suggests how possibly well-intentioned educators justified the segregation to themselves, and the racism that was nonetheless behind it:

> I have noticed that the Spanish speaking children are unusually gifted in music, above the American children, and I believe that phase of their talents ought to be developed . . . and in art, on an average, I find they are superior to the American child in this talent, and I believe their work should include art and a good deal of handicraft work at the first grade. By nature I feel they are endowed with special facilities for this work.
>
> So far as mentality is concerned there is no perceptible difference in the mentality of children of Spanish or Mexican descent . . . but there is a little difference in temperament and a difference in certain talents.

He asserted that "in mathematics they are very apt where the language difficulty does not obtain, and often make more progress than the American children," and added, "I have been told that it is true that a Mexican child will reach the puberty stage sooner than an American child, and that people originating in torrid climates will mature earlier; it's owing to the climatic conditions." The assumption that Mexican-Americans were biologically distinct, of course, echoed the claims being made about African-Americans in the segregated South.

The district admitted that the relatively few Anglo migrant students who began the year late were not segregated. District court judge Joseph Jones therefore ruled that the Mexican children were entitled to go to school with the Anglo children. The case ultimately went to the Texas Court of Civil Appeals, which overturned Judge Jones's ruling.

Some of the appeals court's language reflects the belief of the Anglo community that all was well in its world, occasional complaints notwithstanding. Sometimes assuming that Mexicans belonged to the white race, sometimes indicating that perhaps they did not, the court stated:

> It is to the credit of both races that, notwithstanding widely diverse racial characteristics, they dwell together in friendship, peace, and unity, and work amicably together for the common good and a common country. Racial dissensions, if any occur, are so rare and slight as to escape public notice. . . . It is a matter of pride and gratification in our great public educational system and its administration that the question of race segregation, as between Mexicans and other white races, has not heretofore found its way into the courts of the state.

School officials could not segregate Mexican-American students solely because of their ethnic background, the court held. It was, however, the duty of school authorities — indeed, it was "the very essence of the science of teaching" — to "classify and group the pupils as to bring to each one the greatest benefits according to his or her individual needs and aptitudes." If the authorities' decisions occasionally ruffled parents' "sensibilities," their recourse was to those authorities.

Courts could interfere "only when the school authorities go clearly beyond their administrative powers," which would be the case if decisions to segregate were made on the basis of race. The reasons for segregation given by the superintendent, "if impartially applied to all pupils alike" and "applied in good faith . . . with no intent or effect to discriminate against any of the races involved," were reasonable. The segregation at issue would be unlawful "if the rules for the separation are arbitrary and are applied indiscriminately to all Mexican pupils in those grades without apparent regard to their individual aptitudes or attainments, while relieving children of other white races from the operation of the rule." Assignment to specific schools would be illegitimate "to the extent that the classification is arbitrarily imposed upon those of one race, but relaxed in its application to those of the other races." In other words, assignment had to be made on the basis of individual abilities.

The court found that there was no indication in the record that assignment was made on any other basis, so it voided Judge Jones's injunction. With the mildest of slaps on the wrist, the school authorities were permitted to keep their system intact. Salvatierra asked the U.S. Supreme Court to review the case, but it declined to do so. The attorney general of Texas issued an opinion stating that segregation of Mexican children was illegal when based on race and that segregation was permissible only if unbiased tests indicated language deficiencies. He did not establish an enforcement mechanism, and the directive was widely ignored. Subsequent challenges to the continued segregation got nowhere. Like California, Texas was not ready for the integration of Mexican-American schoolchildren.

The victory, then, was not much of one. By quoting the school superintendent's description of the differences between "children of Spanish or Mexican descent and those of Anglo-Saxon parentage" at great length, the court implicitly accepted the idea that such differences did exist and that they were the result of the culture in which the Mexican children had been raised. Race-based segregation was unacceptable, but segregation based on cultural differences was lawful. Culture became a proxy for race, and the children's "individual needs and aptitudes" that could legitimately be taken into account when placing them in classrooms clearly included their ancestry.

The cash-poor and understaffed LULAC temporarily gave up on

the legal system as a route to reform. Its members were encouraged to try negotiating with local school districts instead. As noted earlier, this approach had very limited results.

By the 1940s, then, Mexican-Americans were well integrated into the economy of Southern California but were kept largely at the lowest income levels. When Robert M. La Follette Jr., chair of a subcommittee of the U.S. Senate's Committee on Education and Labor, undertook an investigation of California agriculture in 1938, he found that the industry was dominated by huge corporate farms. Seven percent of California's farms owned 42 percent of all farmland, other large farms owned much of the rest, and the great majority of farmworkers labored for hourly wages. By 1940, Mexican immigrants and their American descendants were almost 100 percent of the picking force. The census of 1940 recorded 134,000 foreign-born Mexicans in California, 220,000 U.S.-born Mexican-Americans of foreign or mixed parentage, and 64,000 Mexican-Americans born in the United States to Mexican-American parents. They remained the victims of discrimination and racism both on and off the farms. Mexican-Americans were not chosen for juries. They were not welcome in places of public accommodation such as movie theaters and swimming pools — or, if they were permitted in, they were restricted to the balconies of the movie houses and special "Mexican days" at the pools. Restrictive covenants prevented them from moving into better, "white" neighborhoods. Their communities were vibrant but, for the most part, politically inactive.

The relationship of Mexican-Americans to their adopted country was about to change, however. One reason was the hope generated by President Franklin D. Roosevelt's New Deal and its concern for justice and social equality. In 1941 Roosevelt issued an executive order establishing the Committee on Fair Employment Practices (CFEP), which prohibited discrimination on the basis of "race, creed, color, or national origin" by businesses with federal government contracts. Neither the New Deal nor the CFEP generated substantial economic or political gains for Mexican-Americans, but the idealism they reflected resonated with Mexican-Americans and gave them a sense of connection to the federal government. Another reason for the changing relationship was the thinking of the Mexican-American children of the immigrant generation. Born and raised in the United States, and becoming adults in the late 1930s and early 1940s, they had gone to American public schools, learned American values, and watched the struggles of Mexicans and Mexican-Americans in the field of labor. They were ready to assert their rights as Americans.

An equally important factor was World War II. After Japan bombed Pearl Harbor in 1941 and the United States entered the war, there was a tremendous demand for soldiers and laborers. Estimates vary, but it is clear that substantially more than 300,000 and perhaps as many as 500,000 Mexican-American men, many of them from California, were drafted or enlisted in the armed forces. They served with distinction, receiving twelve Medals of Honor along with other awards, including the Silver Star, Bronze Star, Distinguished Service Cross, Distinguished Flying Cross, Navy Cross, and Purple Heart. More than 9,000 Mexican-Americans were killed in action. Like the veterans of World War I, many of those who survived returned home determined to end discrimination. One former paratrooper would tell the *Santa Ana Register* years later, "We'd just been at war. We didn't like it when we came home and found out we'd risked our lives, but now we weren't treated equally and that our children wouldn't be getting as good an education as the white student was going to be getting. It seemed grossly unfair." Santa Ana veterans created the Latin American Organization (LAO) in 1943, its purpose being to combat school segregation. They were typical of the veterans returning home to California who would gradually take over the leadership of their communities from the more quiescent immigrant generation that preceded them. LAO's first act was to encourage William Guzmán, a Santa Ana resident, to ask the school board to permit his son Billy to attend the Anglo school. The board did not bother to respond, and Guzmán would become a plaintiff in *Mendez*.

Mexican-American veterans were welcomed back by a community well aware of their sacrifices and achievements. "We're tired of being pushed around," a teenager wrote to George Sánchez, a leading scholar and activist, in 1943. "We're tired of being told we can't go to this show or that dance hall because we're Mexican or that we better not be seen on the beach front. . . . My people work hard, fight hard in the army and navy of the United States. . . . They're good Americans and they should have justice." It was a feeling shared by many Mexican-Americans.

It was not shared by all other Americans, however. In Los Angeles, local newspapers wrote of the perceived threat posed by the *pachuco* (a term derived from the slang name for the border crossing town of El Paso) "zoot suiters" in the early 1940s. The disenchanted young Mexican-American men had taken to strutting around in an outfit that consisted of a broad-brimmed hat, a fingertip-length jacket, and draped trousers that were wide at the knees and tapered at the ankles. The zoot suits were topped off by long hair worn in a ducktail. In August 1942 young José Díaz was found seriously wounded not far from Sleepy Lagoon, a swimming pit in East Los Angeles, following a fight at a party between a zoot-suited gang and party guests. Díaz died later that night. Police jailed the entire gang, beat many of its members, and charged twenty-two of them, aged sixteen through twenty-two, with criminal conspiracy. They were paraded before the grand jury without being permitted to wash, change their clothes, or cut their hair. In January 1943 an all-Anglo jury found seventeen of them guilty of crimes ranging from assault to murder, after a trial that lasted for thirteen weeks (*People v. Zamora*). The trial judge permitted the defendants to be marched into the courtroom en masse. There they were seated away from their lawyers so they could not consult them. In addition, the seating arrangements frequently made it impossible for the defense lawyers to hear and see what was happening. The judge repeatedly demeaned the defense team and their clients in front of the jury. The proceedings were so unfair that Carey McWilliams, a lawyer, writer, and activist who became chair of the Sleepy Lagoon Defense Committee, described them as "more of a ceremonial lynching than a trial in a court of justice."

The verdict was appealed, and a number of civil rights and labor groups submitted an *amicus curiae* ("friend of the court") brief, contending that racial discrimination had kept the defendants from receiving a fair trial. One of the lawyers on the brief was A. L. Wirin, who would figure in *Mendez*. The Second District Court of Appeals overturned the convictions in October 1944, chastising the trial judge as it did so. McWilliams called the decision the first such major victory for Mexican-Americans.

Nonetheless, in 1943, Los Angeles newspapers ignored the questionable trial proceedings and called for a campaign against "zoot-suit hoodlums." Five months after the convictions were handed down, there were ten days of clashes between Mexican-American youths and Anglo servicemen, joined by some Anglo civilians. Servicemen attacked and stripped clothes from young Mexicans in East Los Angeles, dragging them out of movie theaters and chopping off their hair while the police stood by. The Zoot Suit Riots, as they were dubbed by the media, became so violent and generated so much negative international coverage during wartime that the American government felt compelled to declare Los Angeles off-limits to soldiers and sailors.

The Sleepy Lagoon case and the Zoot Suit Riots demonstrated both the new ideas about justice that were circulating during World War II and the great distance that remained between Mexican-Americans and equality. On one side there were Anglos like Carey McWilliams, the defendants' lawyers, clergymen, and professors, as well as Hollywood stars such as Rita Hayworth, Henry Fonda, and Orson Welles — the stars having been recruited for the Sleepy Lagoon Defense Committee by McWilliams, who was savvy enough to understand the value of publicity. All professed outrage at the discrimination against American citizens, whatever their ethnicity. On the other side were the Los Angeles press, with its rabble-rousing depictions of Mexican-American youth; the clearly prejudiced police and trial judge; and the rampaging servicemen. They were joined in spirit by the growers who exploited Mexican-American farmworkers, the owners of movie houses who denied them entry, the city fathers who banned them from parks and swimming pools, and the school officials who considered their children unfit to attend school with other children and prepared them only for a life of drudgery.

By the 1940s, however, the theories of the educators who advocated segregation for Mexican-American students were being challenged. Some of the challenges actually dated back to the 1930s, although they had been largely ignored then. George I. Sánchez, director of information and statistics for the New Mexico Department of Education as well as a scholar-activist, stated then that the children's lesser achievements reflected their environment and their being shunted into inferior "Mexican" schools rather than a lack of ability. Hershel T. Manuel of the University of Texas said the cause was poverty and bilingualism, not biology. Such criticism of the older theories became more insistent toward the end of World War II. After all, the country had been fighting Hitler, whose racist beliefs led to the creation of concentration camps. Eugenics – the theory that the inherited, undesirable traits of "lesser" human beings could be eliminated by discouraging carriers of those traits from reproducing and encouraging reproduction by others – had been popular in the country during the early decades of the twentieth century, but it, too, was losing credibility.

The new thinking of some educators was notable. In 1945 the California Elementary School Principals' Association published its annual yearbook under the title *Education for Cultural Unity*. In the introduction, University of California provost Monroe E. Deutsch lamented that "the fires of racial and religious intolerance are being fanned in California" and asserted that teachers, along with others, had an obligation to do something about it. Anthropologist Harry Joijer wrote in the yearbook that racial differences were a function of "inherited physical variations" and did not by themselves determine anyone's mentality or aptitudes. "It is evident," he added, "that conflict between groups differing in racial type or in cultural traditions is a deterrent, not an aid, to the progress of civilization." Helen Heffernan, head of the state Department of Education's Elementary Education Division, observed that Mexican-American children, as members of a minority group, were faced with a "serious social adjustment" to school and to a new language. The problem was "complicated" by segregation, which "has almost completely misfired" and which "represents a practice which schools should endeavor to eliminate gradually." Forecasting an argument that would be made both in *Mendez* and later in *Brown v. Board of Education*, Heffernan asserted that "segregation is destructive of the sound mental health of minority people because it produces feelings of insecurity, inadequacy, and separation from the social group." Perhaps most surprising for the time, Heffernan was sufficiently astute to note that segregation had "equally detrimental effects upon the dominant group," fostering "provincialism" and preventing an "enrichment of experience."

This was the thinking of an elite, however, and it was far from typical of the attitudes held by most California educators. University of Chicago anthropologist Allison Davis, one of the first African-Americans to hold a full-time position at a "white" American university, had studied thirty-three California public schools. His article in the 1945 yearbook reported that in California, "almost all teachers believe . . . that the social habits and attitudes of Mexican and Negro Americans are inherited, or racial." Although "every important authority on the testing of intelligence . . . has pointed out that the available tests may not be used legitimately to compare the abilities of children who come from clearly different social and cultural environments," the tests were nonetheless used routinely throughout the state. "Teachers use this 'scientific' judgment, as symbolized in the IQ, to justify the schools' discrimination against colored pupils, and their own inefficient teaching." He excoriated the practice of limiting "Negro, Mexican, and Chinese Americans to only certain trades courses, and to 'maid's' work courses."

Yet even Davis, who lamented that teachers were ignorant of the "culture, and social psychology" of minority groups, urged that schools be desegregated because "to learn the culture of American native whites, the Mexican, Negro, and Chinese-American children must have contact with American white children in the public schools." Nothing was said about teaching the "native white" Americans about the cultures of other groups. It appears that even educators who considered the segregation of Mexican-American students a mistake assumed that integration would be based on Americanization and the subsequent decline of Mexican culture and the Spanish language.

Other members of the American elite were also paying new attention to Mexican-Americans, and this included officials in Washington. President Franklin D. Roosevelt, uneasy about relations with Latin America, began the Good Neighbor policy early in his administration. It included attempts to change the relatively negative image of Latin America and its citizens in the American mind. By the time World War II began, Roosevelt was concerned about securing Latin America in general and Mexico in particular as allies, in part because of the shared border between Mexico and the United States. The United States also needed Mexican products such as copper and lead for the war effort. Official attitudes toward Mexico were altered as well by the fact that when American men marched off to war, they left behind jobs that needed filling. One result was a pact the U.S. Department of Agriculture concluded with Mexico in 1942, bringing *braceros* — migrant agricultural workers — to the United States. The Mexican government's awareness of discrimination against Mexican-Americans led it to include a clause in the agreement stating: "Mexicans entering the United States as [a] result of this understanding shall not suffer discriminatory acts of any kind."

The federal government's interest in improving the lot of Mexican-Americans in order to enhance the United States' status abroad dated from at least 1940, when the Roosevelt administration created the Office of Inter-American Affairs (OIAA) in the State Department. Nelson Rockefeller, later governor of New York and vice president of the United States, was named coordinator of inter-American affairs in 1940 and saw the OIAA's mandate as including work on behalf of Mexican-Americans. In late 1941 officials of the OIAA expressed concern about "repercussions in Latin America" over discrimination against Mexican-Americans. Negotiations over the *bracero* program, as mentioned earlier, gave the Mexican government an opportunity to raise the question of discrimination. As historian Gilbert González has shown, the fear of Nazi propaganda in the countries south of the United States, as well as the wartime need for Latin American raw materials, made the Roosevelt administration eager to placate governments and populations in those nations.

Rockefeller therefore created the Division of Inter-American Activities in the OIAA in March 1942, charging it with the task of promoting interethnic understanding. Lobbied by activists in the Southwest, the division in turn established a Spanish and Portuguese Speaking Minorities Section to fight discrimination. The director of the division in fact went to Los Angeles in 1942 to try to lessen the widespread discrimination against Mexican-Americans that was evident in the Sleepy Lagoon case, although with negligible success. George I. Sánchez, by then a past president of LULAC as well as a faculty member at the University of Texas, had been in communication with Roger Baldwin, executive director of the American Civil Liberties Union (ACLU), about possible litigation against Texas school segregation. "I have seen some of your friends in Washington lately," Baldwin wrote to Sánchez in late 1942, "and they think it would be very opportune to raise these issues now for their effect on Latin America." Sánchez himself was appointed educational consultant to the OIAA in 1943. The federal government's efforts to maintain good relations with Mexico and the rest of Latin America, and to minimize discrimination that might lead to social unrest at home, continued throughout the war.

None of that had a major impact on the thinking of many Anglos in California. The labor shortages of World War II had brought more and more Mexicans to work in the state, and many other Californians viewed them and their Mexican-American counterparts with suspicion. The "fires of racial and religious intolerance" cited by Deutsch in the educators' yearbook were also fueled in part by reactions to the large number of African-Americans who had arrived to work in the state's war industries. The cultural climate, in other words, was changing — but the process of change was still in its early days. Mexican-Americans had little reason to feel accepted by the larger California populace.

That was not going to stop Gonzalo and Felícitas Méndez.

CHAPTER 3

The Parents Decide to Sue

*The reason usually advanced for segregation is that of linguistic difficulty.
It seems a queer one to advance in a country which has educated millions of
second-generation children, speaking all sorts of foreign tongues, without
recourse to segregation.*

RUTH TUCK

Gonzalo Méndez was born in the Mexican state of Chihuahua in 1913.
He and his family became part of the wave of Mexicans migrating in
the first decades of the twentieth century, moving to the United States
in 1919. One of Méndez's brothers, under threat from the regime of
Pancho Villa, came first; he was soon followed by Méndez's mother
and her four other children. They landed in Westminster, California,
where Mrs. Méndez's sister was already living. There, Gonzalo was
sent to the Westminster Main School, along with other Mexican and
Anglo children in his school district. He had reached the fifth grade
by 1927 or 1928 (he was not sure, later, of the date), at which time he
and his schoolmates found out that grades three through five were
being segregated, and the Mexican students would attend classes in a
new building on the same grounds as their former school. The new
school was a small frame building; the old one, a larger building fac-
ing a playing field. Lawyer-activist Carey McWilliams, who wrote a
history of Mexican-Americans, described the Anglo Westminster
school as "handsomely equipped," with "green lawns and shrubs,"
whereas the "Mexican" Hoover School had "meager equipment [that]
matches the inelegance of its surroundings."

Méndez remembered that he and about ten other fourth- and fifth-
grade boys whose English was good were transferred back to their old
school after about three months. Méndez soon had to drop out, however, because his mother ran out of funds and he had to go to work to
help support the family.

The search for a livelihood took him to the fields, where he became
known as a champion orange picker. One of his fellow field hands was

Felipe Gómez, who had migrated to the mainland from Puerto Rico in 1926. Gómez and his family, including his daughter Felícita (known as Felícitas), moved first to Arizona, where the Arizona Cotton Growers Association had arranged for hundreds of Puerto Ricans to pick cotton. The working and living conditions proved so onerous, however, that the migrant workers staged protests and ultimately dispersed. After six months the Gómezes, like many of the other disenchanted families, moved to California. Their first stop was San Bernardino, but they subsequently followed Gómez's work on the railroads to Lancaster, Palm Springs, and White Waters. They eventually settled in Westminster's Mexican neighborhood, where Gómez went to work picking eggplant and encountered Méndez.

Gómez invited the young Méndez to his home, and that is where Gonzalo met Felícitas. They were married in 1935, and after working together in the fields for three years, the couple opened the Arizona Café in the Mexican barrio of Santa Ana. They prospered during the early years of World War II, accumulating sufficient funds to purchase three houses. Méndez had always wanted to try his hand at running a farm, however, and in 1943 their banker told them about the Munemitsus, a Japanese-American family that had been "relocated" to an internment camp. The Munemitsus knew that Japanese-American owners were likely to lose possession of their untenanted farms and to find it difficult if not impossible to reclaim them, and they were worried about their family farm in Westminster. Would the Mendézes be interested in leasing the farm until the Munemitsus were able to return? Gonzalo and Felícitas traveled to Arizona, where the Munemitsus were being interned, and the two families signed an agreement.

The Méndezes closed the café, rented out their house in Santa Ana, and moved to Westminster. They took Frank Vidaurri and his family with them. Vidaurri, married to Méndez's sister Soledad, had experience operating a farm, and Méndez thought Vidaurri would make a good foreman. The two families began running the 40-acre Munemitsu asparagus farm, which employed fifteen workers for most of the year and as many as thirty—including *braceros*—during the peak season. In addition, Gonzalo worked as the foreman of a second farm that grew asparagus on 22 acres and chili peppers on another 100, along with avocados and oranges in a nursery. There, he supervised ten workers in the asparagus fields, in addition to another twenty-five to forty who came and went, depending on the season. Gonzalo was in charge of marketing all the asparagus as well as keeping many of the farm's books. "You are what we would call a dirt farmer, then, in charge of the other dirt farmers there?" the judge in the *Mendez* case would ask him. "Yes, your Honor," Méndez replied. But he was no longer the average Southern California Mexican-American field hand; he had become a relatively well-off farmer.

When Méndez first decided to apply for American citizenship, before he was married, he discovered that the wait for citizenship papers was two or three years. Knowing that he would soon be the husband of an American citizen and that the wait for the spouse of an American was only six to nine months, he held off. Although he applied as soon as he and Felícitas were married, his application was returned. The photographs were not the right color and size, he was informed, and the authorities needed clearer proof of his having been born in Mexico. He was finally naturalized two years before the *Mendez* case went to court, when he was thirty years old.

By then, the Méndezes had three children: Sylvia, who would be nine years old when the trial began in 1945; Gonzalo Jr., eight years old; and Jerome (called Gerónimo by his father), age seven. They grew up speaking English as well as Spanish, and in fact, the family spoke more English than Spanish at home. Méndez fully expected that the children would attend his old school, the Westminster Main School, also known as the 17th Street School. He and Felícitas were busy working the farm on the morning the children were supposed to register for school, which is why his sister took them along with two of her own children. What he did not realize was that in the intervening years, segregationist attitudes had hardened, and the separation of Anglo and Mexican-American children was almost total.

The Méndez and Vidaurri families were the only Mexican-Americans in their neighborhood. Méndez estimated that his neighbors consisted of perhaps fifty Anglo families, and all their children went to the Westminster Main School. Méndez was therefore appalled when his children came trooping home and told him that they would have to go to the Hoover School, which was located in a different school district and whose 152 pupils were all Mexican or Mexican-American. Felícitas was equally infuriated, outraged as she already was by segregation. "I was a citizen, born a citizen in Puerto Rico," she would tell an interviewer years later. "I could not even go to a theater and sit with the other people." They decided that if the children's only choice was to attend a segregated school, they would go to no school at all.

Gonzalo went to the Westminster school the day after his children were turned away and spoke to the principal, but his children were still not permitted to register. The following day he went to the Westminster school board, where he was equally unsuccessful. Eventually he went to the Orange County school board, again to no avail.

These failures made the Mendézes no less determined to end what they saw as a flagrant injustice. Their determination may have stemmed in part from Méndez's own years at the Westminster school, Felícitas's knowledge of her rights as an American, and their awareness of their compatriots' bravery in labor organizing and in war zones. Perhaps the Méndezes knew as well about grassroots anti-desegregation efforts in Southern California, such as the boycotts of segregated movie houses in nearby Ontario, which were well publicized by the popular Spanish-language weekly *El Espectador*. The human rights ideas fostered by World War II were affecting many Mexican-American parents. By 1945, parental action had led the Ontario school board to discuss integration, and there were protests in San Bernardino, Mendota, and Riverside as well. None of those protests, however, resulted in litigation. In any event, the Méndezes decided to fight. They knew the battle would have to go through legal channels, but they were at a loss as to where to turn. Henry Rivera, their produce truck driver, suggested that they see attorney David C. Marcus. The Mexican consulates in Los Angeles and San Diego were among Marcus's clients, and Rivera had read in the local newspapers that Marcus had recently won an important case involving the San Bernardino public swimming pool.

Like other Southern California municipalities, San Bernardino declined to permit Mexican and Anglo citizens to swim together, and it was not alone in doing so. The nearby town of Orange, for example, had "Mexican Day" on Mondays, when Mexicans and Mexican-Americans were permitted to use the public pool. Each Monday night the pool was drained. It was closed on Tuesdays for cleaning and refilling, after which it was considered fit for use by Anglos. San Bernardino dealt with the issue by refusing Mexican-Americans any admission whatsoever to the town's only public park and swimming pool. In September 1943 it denied access to Ignacio López, an American citizen, graduate of the University of Southern California, World War II veteran, translator for California's Division of War Information, and editor of *El Espectador*. San Bernardino also kept out the Reverend R. N. Núñez, parish priest at the Guadalupe Church; Eugenio Nogueroa, a Puerto Rican veteran, editor, and publisher; and two students. Their repeated protests to various city officials were to no avail. They turned to David Marcus, who brought the case of *Lopez v. Seccombe* on their behalf and that of 8,000 other San Bernardino citizens "of Mexican and Latin descent and extraction." The defendants in the class-action suit were W. C. Seccombe, the mayor, along with the city councilmen, chief of police, and park superintendent.

/The plaintiffs were fortunate in having Judge Leon Yankwich of the federal district court in Los Angeles assigned to the case. Yankwich was an immigrant from Romania who, as he said a few years later, viewed American law as based on the principles of liberty, equality, and "the limitation of the power of authority." "The concept of equality," he stated in a book he wrote about the American Constitution, "stems from the principle of the worth of every man." In 1944 Yankwich found for the plaintiffs. He cited the U.S. Constitution's Fourteenth Amendment, which states in part, "No State shall . . . deny to any person within its jurisdiction the equal protection of the laws." Yankwich read that to mean that the states and their municipalities had to treat people equally, giving them equal access to whatever facilities the state created. He therefore issued a permanent injunction prohibiting San Bernardino from keeping its Mexican-American residents out of the pool. Told about Marcus's victory, Méndez arranged to see the attorney at his Los Angeles office.

There Méndez found a dapper man of average height with olive skin, brown eyes, and a well-groomed mustache. Marcus was the son of immigrants himself, his father, Benjamin Marcus, having immigrated to the United States from Tblisi, Georgia. Benjamin initially supported himself and his family by peddling goods throughout the Midwest and later founded stores in Albuquerque and Los Angeles. David, the oldest of his five sons, was born in Iowa in 1904. He went to elementary school in Des Moines and high school in Albuquerque, where his family had moved in the hope that the desert climate would help his mother's tuberculosis. Marcus's brothers left school to open businesses in Los Angeles. Marcus, however, wanted to go to college, although his educational career proved to be a somewhat checkered one. He entered the University of New Mexico as an engineering student but, unhappy in his studies, flunked out. He then attended the University of California at Los Angeles, where he played football until he was kicked in the face and had his chin split open, at which point his father made him give up the sport. He graduated from the University of Southern California's law school in 1927, worked briefly for the Mexican consulate in Los Angeles, and then opened the single-practitioner private practice he would maintain for the rest of his life.

Marcus had experienced anti-Semitism on his road to becoming an attorney. One of the stories he told his children was about his desire, as a violin-playing teenager, to participate in a recital. He was permitted to play, but he had to do so from behind a curtain, as the organizers would not allow a Jewish performer to be seen. He found the University of Southern California of the 1920s to be anti-Semitic as well. His children believed that these snubs sensitized Marcus to the discrimination suffered by others and were responsible for his involvement in civil rights cases.

Marcus's 1926 marriage to Esther Rosenthal produced a son but lasted only two years. Marcus then married Maria Yrma Davila, a Mexican immigrant of Portuguese and Spanish heritage. Her father, who had been educated in France, was the doctor to one of Mexico's presidents. Dr. Davila and his family were among the Mexicans who fled to the United States because of political upheaval, and the teenaged Maria Yrma arrived speaking no English. She quickly became fluent, however, and she and David Marcus raised their children to be bilingual. Marcus's Spanish, described by one of his daughters as "bearable," became good enough for him to be able to translate for clients in the courtroom.

Marcus specialized in immigration and criminal law. His office suite was frequently crowded with clients, many of them Mexican. Like other lawyers who handled civil liberties and civil rights cases, Marcus balanced such relatively unremunerative cases with others that produced greater income, and his practice thrived. The family first lived in Baldwin Park, then a farming community outside of Los Angeles, where his children went to public school. In 1946, when Gonzalo and Felícitas Méndez were fighting to have their children properly educated, Marcus too was the father of public school students. By that time, Marcus had bought the Pasadena mansion where he would live for the rest of his life. His family remembered it as having a tennis court and a swimming pool, a chauffeur and a gardener, quarters off the kitchen for the live-in Mexican servant couple, and "bathrooms which were so big they were almost the size of a small room." Musicians and artists were guests on the weekends. The Marcuses' daughters, Maria Dolores and Norma, clad in white gowns and white lace mantillas and carrying pink camellias, were introduced to society at the 1952 Las Damas Pan Americanas Debutante Ball.

Perhaps his wealth enabled Marcus to take on the San Bernardino swimming pool case and the *Mendez* case, as well as others involving poor immigrants and people caught up in the criminal justice system; perhaps he would have done so in any event. Little is known about Marcus's cases because two of his daughters destroyed his papers shortly after his death. What is known is that Marcus told Méndez about the California education law that permitted the segregation of other children but did not mention Mexican-Americans. Marcus suggested that Méndez's case would be stronger if he were able to prove that not only Westminster but other school districts in Orange County as well segregated Mexican-American students. Was there evidence of that?

The farmer and the man who was now his lawyer determined to find out. The way to do so was to begin contacting Mexican-Americans in other communities. With Méndez driving, the two men roamed the county, interviewing parents and pulling evidence together. Fred Ross, who was a fieldworker for the American Council on Race Relations and a disciple of Chicago grassroots organizer Saul Alinsky, and Hector Tarango, secretary of the Latin American Council and editor of the weekly *Latin American*, went from family to family, trying to identify potential plaintiffs. Many parents were afraid of repercussions if they became involved; some were content to have their children attend the segregated schools because their location in the *colonias* meant they were close to home. Other parents sponsored meetings to talk about the case. The local Mexican-American organizations that existed declined to back the case, possibly out of a belief that it could not be won, but some individual members were supportive. Méndez, an outgoing man, was well-known in the *colonias* and had been made godfather to a number of children. He threw himself into the case, drawing on his networks and leaving Felícitas to administer the farm for what turned out to be more than a year. It prospered under her management, but Felícitas did more than oversee the farm. As the case progressed, Felícitas organized in the community. She initiated 151 meetings with parents and helped turn their enthusiasm into a group, the Asociación de Padres de Niños México-Americanos, which both provided moral support for the effort and signaled to school officials that the Mexican community was behind the fight.

Méndez and Marcus quickly uncovered the endemic nature of the segregation, as well as the fact that other parents had protested. In Santa Ana, the Sánchez and García families had asked the school board to permit their children to leave the "Mexican" Fremont School and enroll instead in the "American" Franklin School. Their request was denied. On October 25, 1943, Mrs. Leonides Sánchez and Mrs. Frank García (their first names are not mentioned in the minutes) appeared before the Santa Ana school board to protest. The mothers wanted their children to go to Franklin, they told the board, so that they "would have all the advantages of American children and learn to speak English as Americans do." The local attendance officer appeared and admitted that Anglo children were permitted to transfer from Fremont to Franklin. Edith Gilbert, the principal of Fremont, defended the education the children received there, saying proudly that "the older girls are taught to do the cooking" in the school cafeteria. The mothers' request was denied, but the board stated that it would institute a process for "studying on the problem of Mexican children."

The "study" apparently resulted in the board's determination to keep desegregation from happening. Some Mexican-American children had been permitted to stay at Franklin when Fremont had been designated for new enrollees some years earlier. On October 13, 1944, the board decided that set a bad precedent. A form letter dated October 20, 1944, was sent to the children's fathers:

Dear Sir:
At the meeting of the Board of Directors on Friday, October 13th, it was pointed out that certain children at the present time attending Franklin School live in the Fremont School District and have been given special permission to attend Franklin.

Dissatisfaction arises with other parents whose children are not granted the same privilege. We were instructed by the Board of Education to issue notice that your children . . . now attending Franklin School, would be permitted to complete this year there, but that beginning September, 1945 the permit will be withdrawn and they will be required to attend the school serving the district in which you live at that time.

The letter was signed by Harold Yost, secretary of the Santa Ana school board. Yost would be called to testify in the *Mendez* case.

The Sánchezes and Garcías, however, were not willing to wait for a process that they doubted would end up satisfying them. A year after the mothers appeared at the school board meeting, the board discovered that the parents had subsequently used false addresses to enroll their children at Franklin. The November 1944 board meeting, at which great outrage was expressed at the deception, also heard from Santa Ana attorney Charles Martin. As noted in chapter 2, the Latin American Organization had encouraged William Guzmán to ask that Billy, his English-speaking son, be allowed to transfer from Fremont to Franklin. In September 1944 Guzmán made that request, but the principal of the school replied that it was not possible because Billy lived out of the district. The Franklin School was in fact five blocks away from the Guzmán home; the Fremont School, nine; and Guzmán knew that other children from the Fremont district went to Franklin. The principal told Guzmán to speak with Frank A. Henderson, the Santa Ana superintendent of schools. Instead, Guzmán hired Martin to represent him. The Guzmáns were accompanied to the November school board meeting by other families in the Fremont district. As Guzmán would tell the *Mendez* trial court, "Mr. Martin, he did all the talking there . . . he did a lot of talking, but they wouldn't pay any attention to him."

What Martin asked for was the transfer of Billy Guzmán. The board replied that it was "considering district boundary problems" and needed time to decide what to do. Martin agreed to a ninety-day period. When it ended, nothing had been done, and Guzmán joined Méndez in deciding to sue.

The same thing had happened in Garden Grove. Juan Muñoz, who described himself as a "picking foreman in the Garden Grove Citrus

Association," went to the school superintendent's office in September 1941 to ask if his children could go to the nearby Lincoln School instead of the "Mexican" Hoover School. The local Japanese and Filipino children went to Lincoln, he argued, and he asked why his children had to be segregated. Superintendent Harvey Emley's reply, as Muñoz remembered it, was that "the Mexicans were too dirty to go to that school." "Do you object to water?" Emley asked. As Muñoz quoted more of the conversation for the trial court: " 'We had to take the children, the Mexican pupils, and bathe them . . . ,' he [Emley] says, [while] the Japanese and Filipino race was classified higher, a higher race than the Mexican race. He says they was more loyal to this country than the Mexican race. He says, 'They are better qualified citizens than you Mexicans.' " The colloquy continued:

> He says, "The minute the children goes out to the playground, they begin to speak Spanish." He says, "Why?"
>
> I says, "For the simple reason, in the first place, you have discrimination for the Mexican people in segregation, which is one cause to make them believe that their language is Spanish." And I says, "But, Mr. Emley, I have taught my girls already to speak English in the playgrounds while they are in school." I says, "Naturally, I am trying to do all I can."
>
> Then he says, "Well," he says, "the Mexican people come too dirty to school, and they must always have an inspection when we got them, and they must have inspection for tuberculosis in the nurse's room."
>
> "But," I says, "Mr. Emley, that is embarrassing Mexican peoples very much."
>
> Then I told him, "For instance, when you go in front of a class, what do you do?" I says, "Don't you go out there, according to the report of my girl, my oldest girl [his daughter Elena], and go in front of all of the school, and you say, 'All Mexican pupils report to the nurse's room.' You don't say so-and-so and so-and-so. You just say, 'All Mexican pupils,' and right away there is segregation, right there." . . . He had to admit that he called them, "All Mexicans report to the nurse's room for inspection of tuberculosis."
>
> I says, "Couldn't you make it a little change?" And I says, "So that don't embarrass us so much? The Japanese people come here,

and they laugh at us, and the other pupils go by and they stare at them." I says, "My gosh, not all Mexicans are dirty."

Of course, then he told me that they speak Spanish.

Muñoz's children were given no language test, but they still were not admitted to Lincoln, which was five blocks from their home. Instead, they had to go to Hoover, more than a mile away.

There were complaints from other parents of Mexican-American children in the following years, and the September 13, 1944, minutes of the Garden Grove school board state, "Some problems were presented regarding the attendance of Mexican pupils in the schools." The board passed a motion "that a policy be adopted whereby there [shall] be no segregation of schools on a racial basis, but that non-English speaking pupils, so far as practical, should attend schools where they can be given special instruction, that is not necessary for English speaking pupils, and that due regard be given to the proximity of the pupils' residence to the nearest school." In other words, Mexican-American children would be kept within the carefully drawn school districts where they lived, and all would be assumed to be deficient in English.

The story was similar in the nearby town of El Modena, which had two elementary schools named after former presidents of the United States. At the time of the *Mendez* trial, the Roosevelt School, which taught children from kindergarten through eighth grade, had 108 pupils, 83 of whom were described as English-speaking. The lower grades were segregated, however; the 25 Spanish-speaking students were all in the seventh and eighth grades. The school focused on academic subjects. A stucco building complete with pillars and a row of palm trees, Roosevelt was located near El Modena's town center at the corner of Alameda and Chapman streets. The older Lincoln School was on the same grounds, about 120 yards away and separated from Roosevelt by a baseball diamond. It too had classes from kindergarten through grade eight, but they took place in a dark brick building with little foliage.

Lincoln was where the Mexican-American students were sent; in fact, the annual reports of attendance compiled by the Orange County Department of Child Welfare listed the Lincoln School, like the Hoover School in Westminster, as "Mexican." There the children were subjected to regular inspections for fleas and lice and were taught vocational subjects in the school's large basement training shops. Students were permitted to miss the first two weeks of school each year so they could help harvest the walnut crop. When they returned to school, many of them found themselves progressing slowly. A large number were kept in the 1-A class for a year and in the 1-B class for the next year; that is, they spent two years in the first grade, purportedly because their lack of English prevented them from learning more quickly. The same pattern was followed for the second grade. None of their teachers spoke Spanish, the classes were larger than at Roosevelt, and the books were older.

Lorenzo Ramirez had gone to school in El Modena in the 1920s, when there was only one elementary school in the district. He later left El Modena but moved back when he had children of his own. Like Gonzalo Méndez, he assumed his American-born children could go to his old school, so he took three of his sons to enroll in Roosevelt. There he was met by Harold Hammarsten, the El Modena school superintendent, who told him the children would have to go to Lincoln. Ramirez replied that schools should be integrated. "I told him that the days will come when the Japanese, Filipinos and Negroes would be together again," he recalled. Hammarsten expressed doubts about that, but Ramirez continued, "I just told him that I should have rights, and thanks the Lord, we live in a country that everybody was equal, and at the same time that I wanted my kids, or my youngsters, to go among the rest of them, and march through up until the end of the war like the boys be marching right along."

Ramirez was clearly influenced by the service of Mexican-Americans in the armed forces. So, perhaps, were the Lincoln students who had a conversation in May 1945 with the school principal, who was also their eighth-grade teacher. "Some one asked him that we wanted to know why we were separated, the American people, the American children and the Mexican children," Carol Torres remembered. They said "that we were all American citizens, and we didn't see why they had us separated. And he said he just didn't know, he didn't make the rules. That is just what he told us." Her parents had never asked for her to be admitted to Roosevelt: "Well, I guess my father knew very well that they wouldn't admit us over there anyway." Marcus would have Carol Torres testify at the *Mendez* trial.

School segregation was not limited to Orange County. Los Angeles County is to the north of Orange; to its west is Ventura County, the home of Oxnard. A federal court judge read the 1936–1939 minutes of the Oxnard school board as indicating that it "not only established and maintained segregated schools, but also established and maintained segregated classrooms within a school." Later, in 1940, "after considering the matter [of segregation] for a number of years, the Board built the Ramona Schoolhouse 'for the convenience of the Mexican population.' But the conveniences of the Ramona School were few. Its floor consisted of blacktop rolled over bare earth, its illumination came from a single bare bulb, its roof leaked, its toilet facilities were deplorable." Segregation of Mexican-American students was just the way it was throughout California and much of the Southwest. It was not a situation that the Méndezes considered acceptable.

While Méndez and Marcus looked for co-plaintiffs, the Méndezes and their group of parents continued to petition the Westminster board. Felícitas followed the law by taking the children to enroll at Hoover, where they were given no language test. Sylvia Méndez remembered having to eat lunch outside Hoover, which had no cafeteria. The school grounds abutted a cow pasture with an electrified wire fence, which worried her father. Worse, as far as Sylvia was concerned, were the flies, which, attracted by the food, settled on the children and their lunches. The Méndezes frequently kept the children out of the segregated school, and at some point in 1943, Westminster school superintendent Richard F. Harris went to the Méndez home to ask why. "At that time I was a little bit sore, and I didn't want to send my children to the Hoover School," Méndez would tell the trial court. The people nearby were Belgians "who spoke mostly Belgian," along with about fifty Anglo families primarily from Oklahoma, and their children were all permitted to go to the Westminster Main School. Students enrolled at both schools traveled by bus. "Sometimes the bus driver would forget to leave my children there at that stop and would go clear over to the Main School," Méndez complained, "and from the Main School they had to walk about five or six blocks to the Hoover School, whether it was raining or windy, or no matter." Harris told Méndez to speak to the school board.

He did. In August 1944 the Méndezes and Soledad Vidaurri went to a meeting of the board, along with some members of the newly formed Santa Ana Latin-American League of Voters. Gonzalo Méndez, Soledad Vidaurri, and Mr. and Mrs. Peña were chosen as the group's representatives. At least one board member was sympathetic, but no progress was made. The next month, following the advice of David Marcus, the Westminster parents formed an association with Méndez as its head. The Méndezes and a number of other association members promptly went to see Ray Atkinson, the county superintendent of schools in Santa Ana, and presented him with a petition addressed to him and Harris:

> We, the undersigned, parents, of whom about one-half are American born, respectfully call your attention to the fact that . . . segregation of American children of Mexican descent is being made at Westminster, in that the American children of non-Mexican descent are made to attend Westminster grammar school on W. Seventeenth Street at Westminster, and the American children of Mexican extraction are made to attend Hoover School on Olive and Maple Streets. Children from one district are made to attend the school in the other district and we believe that this situation is not conducive to the best interests of the children nor friendliness either among the children or their parents involved. It would appear that there is racial discrimination and we do not believe that there is any necessity for it and would respectfully request that you make an investigation of this matter and bring about an adjustment, doing away with the segregation above referred to. Some of our children are soldiers in the war, all are American born and it does not appear fair nor just that our children should be segregated as a class.

Méndez did most of the talking at the meeting, but Mrs. Peña spoke as well. According to Méndez, "Mrs. Peña related her story, she saying she had two sons in the army and saying she thought it wasn't a very democratic way, on the basis of being that her sons were out there fighting for all of us, and the rest of her other brothers or cousins were out here being segregated as a class." Atkinson said he sympathized with her, and Méndez responded that sympathizing did not do them any good. Mrs. Bermudez added, again in Méndez's words, "that she had lived in San Pedro or Wilmington, either one of those neighboring towns, and that she was not segregated there, and that she wanted her son to have equal rights now that she lived in Westminster; and that she was born here, her husband too, and most . . . of her relatives, were all fighting out in the European theatre during that time, and that she thought that it was not fair nor just to continue on with that segregation there in Westminster and that is why we went there." Superintendent Atkinson agreed that they were rightfully seeking justice but told the delegation that he was merely following board policy. Go see Harris, he advised. They did, and Harris chastised them for failing to vote for a bond issue that had been floated by the board in August 1944.

The bond issue had been touted by the board as a way to improve the schools. It failed by thirty-six votes. As Harris told the Méndez group during their meeting, the funds raised would have enabled the board to put a "health room and a big cafeteria" in the Westminster Main School. Méndez replied that the money would have done nothing for the children at Hoover, who still would have had to eat lunch outside, sitting on the ground. Méndez recalled the conversation at trial:

> That wouldn't benefit us at all, as to your having a nice cafeteria for you here in the Main School . . . while we over there in our Hoover School have nothing but a small building, and without any trees, or benches for my children to come and have their lunch at noon. To the contrary, at noon, when they go out to eat their lunch, they have to sit down on the ground or on the stairs, and the teachers do not even ask our children to go in the room and eat their lunches. . . . They do not care about our children.

Harris later scolded the group because "we did not vote on that school bond election, 'and now you come crying to me and want us to accept your children here at the American school.' He said, 'That is what gets my goat.'" Méndez immediately responded. "I told him that there were a lot of us Spanish boys knew of that voting there, but there had been so many protests during this 15 years that that school was separate there, that a lot of us knew that this was in vain to go and vote to have the Main School be built better, and that that wasn't going to benefit us, we would still be segregated at the Hoover School. Nothing was mentioned that if this bond had gone through that they would have united the two schools."

In other words, the school board claimed that it had been committed to desegregation since 1943 and that the purpose of the bond issue was to expand and improve the Main School so that all the students in the district could go there. Méndez and his colleagues, aware of the district's history, simply did not believe that and asserted that they knew nothing about any plans to unite the schools and desegregate.

Méndez returned to the Westminster school office in October 1944 to speak with Superintendent Harris, who insisted that Mexican children belonged in the Mexican school. They could not be transferred to Westminster Main in any event, he claimed, because so many people had moved to Westminster to work in its war plants that the school was overcrowded. The poorly financed school district could do little to alleviate the conditions. Harris would make an exception to the rule for the Méndez children, however. The Méndezes turned the offer down and replied that their children would stay out of school until the board allowed all the other children in.

Méndez refused to give up. He was back in front of the board on January 16, 1945, by which point the board was discussing unifying the two schools. For the first time, and probably acting on Marcus's advice, he formally asked to have his children transferred from Hoover to Westminster. From a legal standpoint he would be a stronger plaintiff if he could show that his children had been injured by being discriminated against. The board refused, saying that there was no room at Westminster.

Then the larger issue was discussed. "Mr. Gonzalo Mendez expressed the thought to the Governing Board that he and his committee who had visited the School Board September 19, 1944, had not received a definite understanding concerning plans of the School Board for unifying the Hoover and Main School," the minutes of the meeting stated. "It was pointed out again quite clearly to Mr. Mendez that the segregation of the Mexican children from other children was inherited by the present School Board and that they had definite plans to change this situation as soon as the housing problem for such a move could be adequately solved." The board, which by now had probably gotten its own legal advice, seemed eager to dispel any notion that it was responsible for the segregation or that it was caving under the threat of litigation. "Mr. Mendez was informed that the idea of placing all children in one school was not a new topic of the Board and that they had given it serious consideration in October, 1943." The board again pointed out, as it had in September 1944, that if the school bond issue had passed in August, adequate facilities would have been available, and the two schools could have been unified sooner. It added that the move could not take place during the current school term because of insufficient funds.

It is interesting that whatever desegregation plans were under discussion were based on the assumption that the Westminster school would be expanded, in part by moving the Hoover building to the Westminster Main School premises, and all the children in the district would go there. No thought seems to have been given to options that could have been implemented immediately, before any expansion, such as having all the children in specific grades go to Main and having the others go to Hoover. One might postulate that the board was reluctant to send Anglo children to the far less comfortable Hoover building. In any event, it appeared that the board did take the threat of litigation seriously, for it made certain that the minutes of the meeting were sent to Méndez.

Now that the board claimed to have decided to unite the schools, Méndez returned "after the school season" to ask about progress. School board president J. A. Houlihan, who was not unsympathetic, nonetheless told Méndez that the board had to go slow in uniting the schools "because they would create a race prejudice." Méndez was not interested in going slow:

> I told him that still, regardless of everything, that we were going to insist, either by keep going to the School Board meetings, or if we wouldn't get no where by that, that the only thing that was left for us to do would be to sue the School Board of Education. Mr. Houlihan said, "Well, perhaps that will encourage all the people, meaning the Anglo-Saxon race, to speed this school uniting, to unite the schools." And Mr. Youngyoung [a supposedly sympathetic resident who had been brought to the meeting by Méndez], being present at that time, said, "I wouldn't sue the School Board of Education, if I was you."

I said, "If you was me, you wouldn't do it? Would you be satisfied to have your children segregated in a different school?'

"Well," he said, "I don't think so," he said.

"Well," I said, "that is all there is left for us to do."

And after that meeting I haven't gone to another School Board of Education meeting.

Like Superintendent Emley in Garden Grove, Harris alleged that the Mexican-Americans were dirty.

One of the main protests that he put was that most all the Mexican people lived in nothing but shacks, and unsanitary, and that was not sufficient hygienic as to go to the Main School. "How could we send our children, when they were so dirty?" That we should elevate our standard of living up to the standard of living of their race, meaning the Anglo-Saxon race.

I told him that that was impossible for all of us to do so, that I lived on a ranch where Japanese people lived, and houses, we all know they compared to the houses where we live, were equal, and they were admitted to go to the Westminster School . . . he said that the people from Westminster could not, in other words, compete in cleanliness with the American or the Anglo-Saxon people.

Méndez implicitly acknowledged that there was a hygiene problem when he replied that the Westminster association was doing its best to see that the children were clean when they went to school. If they were admitted to Main and were still dirty after that, the superintendent could rightfully complain. At no time, Méndez asserted, did Harris tell the group that the children could not go to Main because they could not speak English. The language question would be a major issue during the trial.

David Marcus had hoped, throughout the conversations with the school boards, that litigation could be avoided. "If your Honor had occasion to know of the meetings that have been held in the various districts of schools" in Orange County, he would tell the trial judge, "it would dissipate your mind that there was any such thought in my mind of promoting such litigation as this." Now, however, Méndez and Marcus were ready to give up on negotiations with the four school boards, as there was no indication that desegregation would take place anytime soon. The Méndezes would provide the bulk of the money for Marcus's fee and for expenses, because the high wartime price of agricultural products had made the farms they ran extremely lucrative. Litigation was nonetheless expensive, and people excited about the case now went door-to-door in the four communities, collecting a dollar at a time.

Before the suit could be filed, however, some basic decisions needed to be made.

CHAPTER 4

Race, Ethnicity, and Trial Strategies

The first decision Marcus had to make was whether to take the *Mendez* case into state court or federal court. A plaintiff normally sues in state court when the claim is that a state law is being violated. Because the California education law permitted the segregation of Indian and Asian students but did not mention Mexican-Americans, Marcus could have argued in state court that the Orange County educators were violating state law by adding a group of people without authority. That approach, however, assuming it was successful, would have left the door open for California legislators to rewrite the law to include Mexicans. And even if Marcus won in the California state courts, the decision would apply only to California. It would have no weight in the other southwestern states that segregated Mexican-American students.

There was an even more persuasive reason not to follow the state court route. Marcus and all the families that would become plaintiffs in the case were troubled by the phenomenon of segregation rather than by the violation of California law. Marcus had been successful in attacking segregation in San Bernardino on the basis of the U.S. Constitution's Fourteenth Amendment, and it was clear that Méndez and the others believed that segregated schools violated both their rights, as American citizens, to obtain for their children the best education offered by the government and their children's rights to have access to that education. If the case succeeded, segregation of Mexican-American children might conceivably be outlawed throughout California and the nation. Initially, a ruling in Méndez's favor would apply only to the four Orange County districts, because the suit would be against the districts and their officials. If the districts appealed that decision, however, and if the losing side in the appeals court decided to take the case further, it could wind up in the U.S. Supreme Court.

Any decision that tribunal handed down would apply to the entire country. The danger, however, lay in the Supreme Court's own precedents, which were binding on all the federal courts. One of the reasons the school districts believed that no court would order them to desegregate was that the Supreme Court had repeatedly ruled that segregation based on race was legal.

In 1896 the Supreme Court held in *Plessy v. Ferguson* that states could require railroads to segregate their passengers by race as long as the accommodations offered to black riders were equal to those offered to whites. The Fourteenth Amendment's requirement that states provide all people with the "equal protection of the laws" meant that people had to be treated equally, the Court said, but not necessarily in the same spaces. The case did not mention other public venues such as restaurants, hotels, parks, or schools. The assumption of southern states, however, was that they had been given a license to separate the two populations in all those places, and subsequent cases did nothing to challenge that view. In *Cumming v. Board of Education*, decided in 1899, the Court declared that school boards could use public funds to establish white high schools even when no schools were provided for black children — which makes one wonder what happened to the "equal" part of the equation. That case was followed by *Berea College v. Commonwealth of Kentucky* in 1908. There, the Court concluded that the Fourteenth Amendment was not violated by a state statute prohibiting schools and colleges incorporated in the state from educating "white" students alongside "negro" students. Other groups could also be segregated. The Court's decision in *Gong Lum v. Rice*, handed down in 1927, declared that a Chinese child forced to attend a school for black children rather than the "white" school was not deprived of the equal protection of the laws.

Some African-American and white reformers reacted to the kind of segregation endorsed by the Court by organizing the NAACP in 1909 to fight discrimination against African-Americans. One of its areas of concern was education, reflecting the organization's belief that segregation resulted in an inferior education that doomed students to an inferior economic status. Charles Houston became the NAACP's first special counsel (chief lawyer) in 1934. Under his leadership, and knowing that a frontal assault on the *Plessy* "separate but equal" doctrine would fail, the NAACP adopted a litigation strategy that would hold states to the "equal" part of the "separate but equal" doctrine. It brought case after case designed to challenge the southern states' provision of highly unequal educational institutions for blacks and whites and, in the case of graduate and professional education, virtually no education at all for black citizens. If the states were forced to expend substantial sums to upgrade and create truly equal schools, the NAACP believed, the cost would convince state authorities that segregation simply did not pay. Its initial efforts were focused on institutions of higher education, in part because they were particularly expensive, and in part because there were almost no such institutions for African Americans in the southern states.

The NAACP brought the case of *Murray v. Pearson* in the Maryland courts. Donald Gaines Murray, a student with good grades from Amherst College, was turned down by the law school of the University of Maryland. The university suggested that Murray apply instead to the all-black Princess Anne Academy, which had no law school. At the time, Thurgood Marshall, the future Supreme Court justice, was a lawyer in private practice working with the NAACP. He and Houston argued in court that Murray had to be admitted to the university's law school because there was no state law school for African-Americans. The trial court agreed with them and, in 1936, so did the Maryland Court of Appeals. The basis for the successful suit, then, was not that segregation was wrong but that the state had to provide equal facilities to qualified black students.

Houston and Marshall went back to court on behalf of an African-American college graduate who had been turned down by the University of Missouri law school. As in Maryland, there was no law school for black students. *Missouri ex rel. Gaines v. Canada* (Canada was the name of the registrar of the university) was appealed all the way to the U.S. Supreme Court, which ruled in 1938 that the state had violated the Fourteenth Amendment's equal protection clause by offering whites but not blacks a law school education. The Court did not consider Missouri's willingness to pay tuition for black students to attend law schools in neighboring states to be an adequate fulfillment of its Fourteenth Amendment responsibility to treat its citizens equally. The NAACP had not argued, and the Court did not hold, that permitting black students to enroll only in a separate but equal facility would violate the Fourteenth Amendment. In fact, the Court wrote that "furnishing equal facilities in separate schools" was "a method the validity of which has been sustained by our decisions." There were, however, no equal facilities here, nor was there any indication that the Court was about to revisit the "separate but equal" doctrine.

The cases the NAACP undertook that involved schooling below the college level by and large emphasized equalizing the pay of teachers and other school personnel. It reported at the end of 1941 that the organization had filed fifteen such suits in the courts during that year. Marshall had become the NAACP's special counsel in 1940. In November 1945, some months after Marcus filed the *Mendez* case, Marshall, not yet having learned about it, sent a memorandum to Roy Wilkins, editor of the NAACP's *Crisis* magazine. The memo indicated that the NAACP's immediate goal in the education field was to compel equality of salaries and facilities. A month later, addressing a Tennessee meeting of the Association of Colleges and Secondary Schools for Negroes, Marshall said, "we believe it is necessary . . . to maintain an active and vigorous campaign to compel absolute equality in educational facilities." The drive was part of a program "seeking to remove all vestiges of discrimination and segregation because of race," but for the moment, the NAACP would concentrate on institutions of higher education and on equalization. In a speech delivered at Howard University in 1952, Marshall declared, "by 1945 plans were ready for a direct attack on the validity of segregation statutes insofar as they applied to public education on the graduate and professional school level." At the end of 1945 he wrote a letter to Carl Murphy, president of the Afro-American Newspapers. "Frankly, and confidentially, and just between the two of us," Marshall told Murphy, "there is serious doubt in the minds of most of us as to the timing for an all-out attack on segregation per se in the present United States Supreme Court."

As David Marcus thought about the approach he would take in *Mendez*, the NAACP — the nation's leading organization dedicated to achieving racial equality — knew without question that desegregation was its goal, but it was not quite ready to mount a frontal attack on segregation below the graduate level.

It had good reasons for not doing so. Not the least of them, according to Marshall's 1952 speech, was that parents of elementary and high school students in the South were realistically afraid of retribution if they challenged any aspect of segregation. He noted as well the constraints created by the NAACP's limited budget. Constance Baker Motley worked for the NAACP, eventually participating in the organization's briefs in *Brown v. Board of Education*, and subsequently became a federal judge. Motley later wrote that right through the 1950s, "no major corporation or foundation was willing to fund so controversial a cause."

In addition, a number of other decisions in the 1940s suggested that the Supreme Court was reluctant to challenge race-based governmental actions. The federal administration decided in 1943, as the country was fighting Japan and the other Axis powers, that West Coast Japanese-Americans constituted a potential fifth column. In *Hirabayashi v. United States* (1943) the Court found no constitutional violation in the federal government's imposition of a curfew on Japanese-Americans as a war measure. The following year it implicitly declared in one case (*Ex parte Endo*) and specifically declared in another (*Korematsu v. United States*) that the system of internment camps to which Japanese-Americans were forcibly removed was constitutional. The country was at war, the Court reasoned, and it would not permit the Constitution to stand in the way of whatever the military believed was necessary to win. The Japanese-American internment was of course the reason why the Méndezes were in Westminster, running the farm for the interned Munemitsu family.

These World War II decisions had nothing to do with education. They did, however, underscore the point that in some situations, the federal courts would uphold governmental actions that differentiated among people on the basis of their perceived race or ancestry. That had to be factored into Marcus's thinking as he and Méndez put together plaintiffs and considered the courtroom strategy they might best employ. The fact that the NAACP still felt the time was not right for an all-out attack on school segregation also must have given Marcus pause.

At the same time, the Court's opinions in *Korematsu* and *Hirabayashi* offered some reason for hope. Justice Hugo Black declared in the *Korematsu* case "that all legal restrictions which curtail the civil rights of a single racial group are immediately suspect. That is not to say that all such restrictions are unconstitutional. It is to say that courts must subject them to the most rigid scrutiny. Pressing public necessity may sometimes justify the existence of such restrictions; racial antagonism never can."

There was somewhat similar language in *Hirabayashi*. "Distinctions between citizens solely because of their ancestry are by their very nature odious to a free people whose institutions are founded upon the doctrine of equality," Chief Justice Harlan Fiske Stone stated. "Classification or discrimination based on race alone has often been held to be a denial of equal protection," he declared, citing the 1886 case of *Yick Wo v. Hopkins*. There, effectively striking down a San Francisco law designed to drive out Chinese-owned laundries, the Court had written, "Though the law itself be fair on its face, and impartial in appearance, yet, if it is applied and administered by public authority with an evil eye and an unequal hand, so as practically to make unjust and illegal discriminations between persons in similar circumstances, material to their rights, the denial of equal justice is still within the prohibition of the constitution." Marcus could argue that the practice of segregating Mexican-American students seemed to be fair because it was purportedly based on language abilities, but in fact, it was "applied and administered by public authority with an evil eye." In addition, the Court had written in *Yick Wo* that if there was no good reason for the law, "the conclusion cannot be resisted that no reason for it exists except hostility to the race and nationality to which the petitioners belong, and which, in the eye of the law, is not justified. The discrimination is therefore illegal, and the public administration which enforces it is a denial of the equal protection of the laws, and a violation of the fourteenth amendment of the constitution." Justice Stone drew on that reasoning to state, "We may assume that these considerations would be controlling here were it not for the fact that the danger of espionage and sabotage, in time of war and of threatened invasion, calls upon the military authorities to scrutinize every relevant fact bearing on the loyalty of populations in the danger areas," and that "racial discriminations are in most circumstances irrelevant and therefore prohibited."

Note that Justice Stone did not use the word *segregation*. He referred instead to *discrimination*. The fact that people were segregated, according to the Court, was not itself proof that they were being discriminated against—and that was precisely why the NAACP concentrated on cases demonstrating that African-American teachers and students were not only segregated but also the victims of discrimination in forms such as poorer classrooms or lack of access to higher education.

The situation of African-Americans was of course different from that of Mexican-Americans, however bad the situation of each. Slavery and discrimination against black people had been part of the nation's history from its inception, and as the violence that followed *Brown v. Board of Education* would demonstrate, many southerners were prepared to fight rather than integrate. One might have argued that undoing the segregation of Mexican-American students, who were far fewer in number than African-American students, would be viewed by a national institution such as the Supreme Court as less threatening. Back in 1945, however, there was no indication whatsoever that the Supreme Court was willing to undo "separate but equal" or to lend a sympathetic ear to the argument that segregating schoolchildren did them harm. Segregation on the basis of race was officially legal, and it was a long-standing part of American history. Would a judicial system that saw no Fourteenth Amendment impediment to the wholesale imprisonment of Japanese-Americans on the basis of their race, not to mention the segregation of and discrimination against African-Americans, be prepared to strike down what it might well see as the lesser evil of segregating Mexican-American students? The answer seemed obvious. What, however, if Marcus argued that *Mendez* had nothing to do with race?

Marcus undoubtedly discussed the case with the local branches of the American Civil Liberties Union (ACLU) and the National Lawyers Guild, because lawyers from those organizations entered the case on Méndez's side. The ACLU, created in 1920, considered its mandate to stem from the first eight amendments to the Constitution and subsequent amendments that expanded the rights of individuals. It was the country's premier civil liberties organization, and its attorneys had been involved in racial equality cases for years. Fred Okrand, who would later become the first legal director of the ACLU of Southern California, and A. L. Wirin, who would become its chief counsel, were in private practice but worked largely without fee on ACLU cases. They and a third attorney had challenged the constitutionality of the Japanese-American internments in the *Korematsu* case, and Wirin had been prominent in the Sleepy Lagoon case. The two men would work with Marcus on *Mendez*. The National Lawyers Guild was founded in 1937 by lawyers disenchanted by the highly conservative positions taken by the American Bar Association, including its acceptance of segregation and its refusal to admit African-American attorneys. The Guild prided itself on being the nation's first racially integrated bar association and on fighting for social justice. Like the Southern California branch of the ACLU, the National Lawyers Guild favored a direct attack on segregated schools.

So did Marcus. He decided to use the Fourteenth Amendment approach, arguing that the segregation of Mexican students deprived them of their federal right to equal treatment by the state. This meant he would turn to the federal court system, which is the proper venue when a plaintiff asserts that a state is in violation of the U.S. Constitution. Because any good attorney uses all the ammunition he or she can muster to best represent the client, Marcus would argue as well that Orange County was violating California law, but the focus of his plea would rest on the Fourteenth Amendment. He filed suit in federal court.

The federal court system is a three-layered one. The U.S. Supreme Court is the top layer. Below it are the federal courts of appeals, all but two of which have authority over specific states. California, as well as Oregon, Washington, Arizona, Montana, Idaho, Nevada, Alaska, Hawaii, Guam, and the Northern Mariana Islands, falls within the jurisdiction of the Ninth Circuit Court of Appeals. That court hears appeals from the federal district courts, which constitute the first, or trial, layer of the system.

The petition David Marcus filed on March 2, 1945, with the District Court for the Southern District of California, located in Los Angeles, carried the names of numerous petitioners and numerous respondents. The petitioners were Méndez and his children Sylvia, Gonzalo Jr., and Jerome; William Guzmán and his son Billy; Frank Palomino and his children Arthur and Sally; Thomas Estrada and his children Clara, Roberto, Francisco, Sylvia, Daniel, and Evelina; and Lorenzo Ramirez and his sons Ignacio, Silverio, and José. As the document said, all the petitioners were citizens and residents in their respective school districts, "and each and all petitioners are of Mexican or Latin descent or extraction." In keeping with the requirements of California education law, the petitioners were also declared to be "of good moral habits, not suffering from disability, infectious decease [*sic*] and are qualified to be admitted to the use of the Schools and facilities within their respective Districts and Systems." The suit was a class action, brought not only for the named petitioners but also on behalf of "some 5,000 other persons of Mexican and Latin descent," all of them citizens and residents of the four districts. As the petition indicated, they shared a "common and general interest," and because they were so "numerous . . . it is impractical to bring all of them before the Court."

The complaint emphasized that the children in the suit were citizens. The Fourteenth Amendment to the Constitution, as noted earlier, states: "No State shall . . . deny to any person within its jurisdiction the equal protection of the laws." This means that citizens and noncitizens alike are guaranteed the equal protection of the laws. Another part of the amendment, however, states: "No State shall make or enforce any law which shall abridge the privileges and immunities of citizens of the United States." Marcus would argue that both clauses had been violated by the school districts.

The respondents — the parties against whom the suit was filed — were the four school districts, their superintendents, and all the members of the school boards. Westminster, Garden Grove, and El Modena were small rural communities; Santa Ana was a city of over 40,000. The basis for the suit, Marcus wrote, was that his clients had been deprived of their rights as American citizens. In carrying out a "common plan, design and purpose" to keep the children from specific schools solely because of their "Mexican or Latin descent or extraction," the districts had violated the petitioners' right to the equal protection of the laws and had caused them "great and irreparable damage." The petitioners asked the court to declare the practice to be unconstitutional and to issue both a preliminary injunction, prohibiting the districts from continuing the practice while the case was being heard, and a permanent injunction.

Some of the language of the complaint is worth reproducing here because it indicates how Marcus tried to get around the problem of the Supreme Court's legitimation of racial segregation:

All children or persons of Mexican or Latin descent or extraction, though Citizens of the United States of America . . . are and have been segregated and required to and must attend and use certain Schools in said Districts and Systems, reserved for and attended solely and exclusively by children and persons of Mexican and Latin descent, while such other Schools are maintained, attended and used exclusively by and for persons and children purportedly known as White or Anglo-Saxon children. . . . [The school districts] have denied petitioners and all others of Mexican or Latin descent from attending and using and receiving the benefits and education furnished to other children residing in said School District and System . . . the injury to petitioners is continuous, great and irreparable [and] is calculated to affect and does affect their health, rights and privileges as citizens of the United States.

Note the words "Mexican and Latin descent." The question at issue, Marcus would insist throughout the litigation, was not whether the four Orange County school districts segregated students on the basis of race. There was no *racial* segregation, he would tell the court, because Mexicans were members of the white race. They were being artificially separated from other students — most of them officially "white" because there were relatively few African-Americans and Asian-Americans in those districts — on the basis of their ethnicity.

Scholars writing in the years after the Chicano movement of the 1960s have criticized assertions in court cases and elsewhere in the 1930s and 1940s that Mexican-Americans were white rather than members of a separate race. For a litigator such as Marcus, however, there was no viable alternative. The Supreme Court of the United States had endorsed racial segregation, so it would have been futile for Marcus to argue in a federal courtroom that segregation based on race was unconstitutional. Besides, the Mexican-American community of the 1940s insisted that it was white. When the Census Bureau had asserted otherwise in 1930, as discussed in chapter 1, the outcry of the community and of the Mexican government had caused the bureau to reverse its decision. The appeals court had written in *Salvatierra v. Del Rio Independent School District* about "Mexicans and other white races." Not being "white" could be dangerous for the Mexican-American community, for it will be remembered that California assemblyman Bliss had tried to write into law his belief that Mexicans and Mexican-Americans were "Indians." Although the legal "whiteness" of Mexican-Americans did not translate into their acceptance by Anglos as equals, their legal status as such meant that at least in that area they could lay claim to full citizenship. One can only wonder what the Méndezes and the other families – not to mention members of his own family – would have thought if Marcus had suggested that they were members of a separate race.

In any event, Marcus understood that he would lose the case if he presented it as one of racial segregation. His obligation was to present the argument that would best serve his clients' chance of winning. That argument was that Mexican-American children were being segregated on the basis of their ancestry – a category that had no relevance to the educational process – so Marcus used the wording "Mexican or Latin descent or extraction" rather than "race." To win, Marcus had to show that the case involved *intraracial* rather than *interracial* segregation. He would, in effect, ask the court to declare that educational segregation within the white race, as opposed to the segregation of different races, was unconstitutional. Supreme Court decisions such as *Korematsu* had upheld different treatment for Japanese-Americans on the basis of perceived needs of national security in wartime. There was no such need when it came to education, and Marcus would seek to prove quite the opposite: that the goal of giving Mexican-American children an education as good as the one provided to other students could not be reached through segregated schools.

When Marcus filed his first papers with the court, the national press paid no attention. The reaction of local papers was mixed. The *Los Angeles Times* barely took notice, printing only a paragraph in its "Los Angeles Briefs" of March 3, 1945, reporting that the suit had been filed. The story was way down in the column, well under an item about a local divorce. The *Orange Daily News* mentioned the case only in a short article, next to a much longer one about growers' organizations asking the War Food Administration to permit them to raise the price of Valencia oranges. The *Santa Ana Register*, however, put the story on its first page, naming all the plaintiffs and defendants. "In his petition, Marcus cited liberally from a book on the Mexican problem by James L. Kent, superintendent of the Garden Grove school district, in which Kent is reputed to have said the reason for segregation was that Mexican children are unable to cope with the American children: that there is a health problem due to malnutrition among many

Mexican children," the story stated. "Kent said he had talked the matter over with the attorney for the plaintiffs recently and had explained to him that most of the children of Mexican extraction start in school without knowledge of English or proper health; that in the first five grades the children are taught to speak the language and are given training in 'morals, manners and cleanliness. . . . As soon as they are able to compete with the Anglo-Saxon children,' the Garden Grove educator said, 'we are only too glad to have them in the classes with the other pupils.'" The other superintendents were also quoted as denying discrimination. One column over, in larger type, the paper carried the story of the marines' bloody battle on the Japanese island of Iwo Jima — a battle that became a turning point in the war as well as an icon of American determination to safeguard democracy. Méndez and the other plaintiffs were trying to safeguard it at home.

The case was assigned to Judge Paul J. McCormick, who, along with many other Californians of his generation, had migrated from the East Coast. McCormick was born in New York City in 1879 and moved to California in 1887. A graduate of public schools in San Diego and Los Angeles, he attended All Hallows College in Salt Lake and St. Ignatius College in San Francisco. McCormick began his legal career in private practice, remaining there until he was appointed a deputy district attorney in 1905. Five years later, Governor James N. Gillette named him to fill a position on the California Superior Court in Los Angeles. McCormick was subsequently elected to the court and then reelected, ultimately serving for thirteen years and adjudicating civil, criminal, and probate cases. President Calvin Coolidge appointed him to the U.S. District Court for the Southern District of California in Los Angeles in 1924, and he remained on that court on active service until 1951.

Off the bench, the judge was deeply involved in Los Angeles society. Then–deputy district attorney McCormick's marriage in 1908 was called "a brilliant event" by the *Los Angeles Times*, which displayed prominent pictures of him and his wife on its society page. Mrs. McCormick's name appeared there frequently in the years that followed — always, in keeping with the custom of the time, as "Mrs. Paul J. McCormick." The newspaper carried pictures of the couple in 1933 when they returned from their annual vacation — that year, a cruise to the South Seas and Tahiti.

Both McCormicks were active in charitable organizations, particularly Catholic charities. The judge was a charter member of the local Knights of Columbus Council; in 1953 the pope would name him a Knight Commander of St. Gregory, one of the highest papal honors for a layman. McCormick's strong moral streak and the importance he placed on religion were reflected in his decisions. In 1923 he was so distressed by what he saw as his duty to pronounce the death sentence on a man convicted of killing a policeman that he consulted his fellow judges beforehand and lamented to the press, "I was consumed with apprehension lest something I had done or said might have influenced the jury in their extreme verdict." "I would wish to be very sure" in handing down a death sentence, he continued. "If you had an atheist on the bench he would hang them all. But a man with any religion must feel the awful, tremendous responsibility of such a task." In 1942, with World War II raging, the judge sentenced a conscientious objector to a year in the county jail. "How are we going to insure free exercise of religion," McCormick asked rhetorically from the bench during the sentencing, "if we don't fight for it?" Some years earlier he had written to the R.K.O. movie production company, deploring films that did not contribute to the "social and moral welfare" and recommending the making of more movies such as *Little Women*.

Any court based in Los Angeles is likely to find itself host to members of the movie community. That certainly was true of Judge McCormick's courtroom, where he presided over relatively mundane citizenship hearings and swearing-in ceremonies but also swore in actors such as George Sanders and Charles Boyer. In 1939 he dismissed a case in which Charlie Chaplin was accused of plagiarizing the movie *Modern Times*. His docket included a full range of civil and criminal cases, and, as in the case of the conscientious objector, his comments from the bench and to the press reflected his beliefs. When he sentenced a Chinese narcotics addict to three years in a federal penitentiary, he said, "It is unfortunate that we have no system of hospitalization for these cases. They are really medical instead of legal problems," thereby indicating that the judge was somewhat ahead of his time. Nonetheless, he demonstrated that in other respects he was very much a man of the moment when he added, with perhaps unconscious racism, "It is particularly vicious to sell narcotics to a white man. Trade in opium between orientals is not as dangerous as this practice." He was firm with people accused of violating Prohibition laws and, as a member of President Herbert Hoover's National Commission on Law Enforcement and Observance, advocated the continuance of Prohibition. He viewed Prohibition's "outstanding good" as "abolition of the legalized open saloon." At the same time, McCormick lambasted what he called the "governmental lawlessness" involved in some Prohibition efforts, especially the tendency of law enforcement officers to search homes without a warrant. McCormick was an avowed Republican but seems to have been a true democrat, with a small *d*. Much as he approved of Prohibition, he suggested that there should be a national referendum on whether to continue the ban on liquor. When, in November 1933, he realized that the Twenty-first Amendment to the Constitution, repealing Prohibition, was likely to be ratified, he advocated setting prices for liquor so that there would be "no need of the bootlegger."

Judge McCormick's service on Hoover's commission brought him national attention. So did the part he played in the notorious Teapot Dome scandal. Huge oil reserves set aside for the use of the U.S. Navy were stored in what were called domes, and the one in Wyoming was dubbed "Teapot Dome" because of the shape of a rock formation in the area. There were two such domes in California, one at Elk Hills. The scandal involved the 1922 bribery of Secretary of the Interior Albert Fall by petroleum companies, as a result of which the companies gained access to the reserves. Word of the transaction got out, and a Senate investigation followed. In 1924, just a few months after McCormick was named to the district court, President Coolidge appointed two special counsels to pursue possible civil and criminal cases resulting from the investigation. One such civil complaint, against the Pan-American Petroleum and Transport Company, was filed in California, and McCormick found himself assigned to it. In 1925 he held that the contract giving the company access to the Elk Hills reserve was void. His ruling was affirmed by the Ninth Circuit Court of Appeals and by the U.S. Supreme Court.

The jurist who would hear the *Mendez* case, then, was a stern moralist, someone whose feelings about racial differences were mixed at best, a man of stature in his community and in judicial circles generally, a firm believer in the Constitution, and, by all accounts, a very pleasant person. Fred Okrand, the ACLU lawyer, remembered him as a "wonderful, really nice man." He was so highly thought of that in 1943 Senator Sheridan Downey, a California Democrat, suggested to President Franklin D. Roosevelt that McCormick be made a judge of the federal Ninth Circuit Court of Appeals, even though McCormick was a loyal Republican. Nothing came of the suggestion, however, so McCormick was the judge assigned to preside over the *Mendez* case in 1945.

On June 4, Judge McCormick scheduled the case for trial on July 5. He ordered the lawyers for both sides to appear before him on June 26 for a pretrial hearing, adding that they were to bring with them all documents relevant to the matter. He was particularly interested in documents that showed "the percentages of English-speaking and foreign-language pupils attending the respective schools." Copies were sent to Marcus; Joel E. Ogle, the Orange County counsel whose office would represent the defendants; George F. Holden, deputy county counsel; and A. L. Wirin and J. B. Tietz, the two ACLU lawyers who would appear as amici curiae. Although Ogle was formally the defendants' attorney, he in fact turned the job over almost entirely to Holden.

Like McCormick, and so many other Californians of the time, Holden came from elsewhere. The Montana native, born in 1897, graduated from the University of Montana Law School in 1923 and migrated to Southern California. He was admitted to the California bar in 1924 and went into private practice. Becoming interested in politics, he served as both an Anaheim city judge and part-time city attorney (Anaheim is in Orange County). Holden ran successfully for the office of Orange County district attorney in 1938. One of the people he appointed to his staff was Joel Ogle, for whom Holden would work in later years. A 1940 photograph in the *Los Angeles Times* shows Holden standing near California attorney general and future U.S. chief justice Earl Warren, who had met with a group of district attorneys from Southern California to discuss law enforcement. That same year Holden served a one-year term as president of the Orange County Bar Association. In October 1942 he appointed Orange County's first woman deputy district attorney. He was defeated when he ran for reelection the following month, although it is unclear whether the appointment contributed to his loss. After working briefly for Douglas Aircraft, he joined the Orange County counsel's office as deputy. Forty-eight years old in 1945, Holden had years of experience in public office and in litigation as he prepared to face the forty-one-year-old Marcus.

It was Holden who appeared for the defense in court and filed all its papers in the case. He began the county's written replies to the complaint by arguing that the district court lacked jurisdiction, which means it did not have the power to hear the case. Federal district courts can hear cases that involve a state's denial of rights that are protected by the Constitution and laws of the United States, and Holden contended that Méndez and the other plaintiffs had not been deprived of any such rights. The answers to the petition that were filed by each of the four school districts on May 4 elaborated on that point.

The quotations that follow are taken from the Westminster district's reply, but all four responses used much of the same language. They acknowledged that the children in the case were constitutionally entitled to equal treatment and maintained that they were getting it. The families "of Mexican or Latin descent" in the district spoke Spanish at home, so their children were "unfamiliar with and unable to speak the English language" when they began school. The districts therefore found it desirable and efficient to educate them separately, the separation being "for the best interests of said pupils of Mexican descent and for the best interests of the English speaking pupils." The Mexican-American students were kept in segregated schools "until they acquired some efficiency in the English language." They were taught by teachers with the same qualifications and salaries as the teachers in the other schools and were given "all of the facilities and all the instruction" available there. The bottom line was that they were being taught separately but equally for sound educational reasons, and they were never separated "solely" because of their ethnicity.

The Santa Ana reply included the information that the district had fourteen elementary schools in fourteen zones, which were based on neighborhoods. The reply unwittingly attested to the drawing of zone lines for the purpose of keeping the children separate. The Fremont, Delhi, and Logan zones, according to Santa Ana's papers, each had a population that was 99 percent "of Mexican descent," and the schools there had "approximately 100 percent" Mexican-American students.

The Wilson, Spurgeon, Hoover, and Jefferson zones had a population and student body that were 100 percent English-speaking. Other zones had varying percentages of distinct populations and student bodies. El Modena had two elementary schools, as did Westminster; Garden Grove had four. The Garden Grove response added that Mexican-Americans in the town lived primarily in their own communities, and "a large percentage of said persons [Mexican-Americans] residing in said communities have not been instructed in or are familiar with the proper rules of personal hygiene."

Marcus and Holden were in Judge McCormick's courtroom at 10:00 on the morning of June 26 for the pretrial hearing, designed to make the trial itself as efficient as possible. During such hearings, the parties' attorneys lay out any areas on which they agree, so that those matters do not have to be covered at trial, and the judge may indicate the particular issues he or she believes should be the focus of the trial. Holden saw no problem in acknowledging, on behalf of the districts, that "the children are taught in different schools practically from the first grade to the sixth grade." As he had said in the answers to the complaint, and as he would argue repeatedly during the trial and the appeal, they were segregated, but not because they were of Mexican descent. And segregation was not discrimination. "We deny that there is any discrimination. We allege that we give them exactly the same education, the same facilities are furnished to them, the same type of teachers are employed as for the other students, and the same courses of instruction are given in those schools."

It was because of residence and zoning rather than malice that three of the Santa Ana schools had students who were "predominantly" Mexican-American, the students in three other schools were what Holden referred to as "white," and those in the remaining eight were largely English-speaking. The same situation existed in the other districts. Marcus replied that the districts "have established certain arbitrary lines which curve and bend and twist to include only those children of Mexican descent," and some children enrolled in the "Mexican" schools had to go straight through the neighborhoods attended by those "of Anglo Saxon descent." Holden disagreed but later admitted that when zoning the Fremont School in Santa Ana, "I believe that they did meander the line a little bit in order to bring in the Mexican people." That was lawful, however, he asserted. "If they were permitted in the same school to segregate them in different classes, then they could segregate them in different school buildings," given "the mental and the other qualifications."

Holden denied as well that there was any conspiracy, saying that each district acted independently of the others. None of the districts had ever ordered the children to be segregated "by race." That brought the subject of race and language about it into the proceedings, and as will become clear, it was a subject that would be handled in conflicting ways throughout the case. Marcus suggested that the two sides might stipulate that, in Santa Ana, the Franklin School was attended only by children "of Anglo Saxon descent" and the Fremont School only by those "of Mexican descent." McCormick disagreed, stating, "The Court wouldn't concur in that. I don't know anything about the antecedents or ethnic or anthropological features of the children, but I wouldn't concur in the Anglo Saxon feature. Undoubtedly, there are Celtic children there." McCormick indicated that he felt more comfortable with language such as "English speaking pupils and pupils of Mexican descent or Spanish speaking pupils"—the formulation used in the breakdown of children submitted by Superintendent Frank Henderson of the Santa Ana district. Looking at that breakdown, McCormick asked if it would be correct to say that in Santa Ana, "children of Mexican descent, regardless of their linguistic qualifications, are not permitted to attend the same school as the [other] children who live within that district attend?"

"No, your Honor, I wouldn't say that," Holden replied, and indeed, that was the thrust of the districts' defense: that the segregation was based on lack of language proficiency rather than ethnicity. Holden continued, asserting that residence in certain zones accounted for the segregation—except when it didn't. He seemed unaware that he was contradicting himself when he stated:

> It happens that the Mexican people live in a certain part of the town, that is, to a large extent, and they have zoned that in a certain way. For example, the Fremont School is in an area where the Mexican people live, so they have zoned it as a school to which the Mexican people or students in that area should attend that school. So the attendance in that school is practically 100 per cent Mexican. . . . Now, I will stipulate to this: That in that district there are

probably between 5 or 10 pupils who are not of the Mexican descent, but are, we will say, English speaking pupils, and they are permitted to go to another school outside of that district. In other words, they don't make those between 5 and 10 pupils attend the Fremont School.

Or, to put it somewhat differently, "English speaking pupils" could opt out of their zoned district; "Mexican" pupils could not. McCormick picked up on that and asked, "Is it conceded that . . . those pupils, if they are of Mexican ancestry or descent, they cannot be permitted to exercise the same choice that the English speaking pupils are permitted to exercise?" Holden was not prepared to concede the point, so Judge McCormick decided that the issue would have to be explored during trial.

Marcus then gave an indication of what one of his arguments would be once the trial began:

> MR. MARCUS: I would like to make inquiry of counsel . . . what he means by Spanish speaking pupils. Does that mean that they only speak Spanish or that they speak both Spanish and English?
> MR. HOLDEN: Of course, it means . . . that they are not efficient in English; in other words, there is a handicap due to language.

Judge McCormick then declared that "if children are segregated solely and exclusively because of their ancestry or lineage, that . . . is an unlawful discriminatory act on the part of the school authorities." Since he knew the Supreme Court had held segregation on the basis of race to be lawful, he presumably had *Hirabayashi* and *Korematsu* in mind when he suggested that segregation on the basis of "ancestry or lineage" rather than race fell into a different category.

The judge was still feeling his way when it came to race and to language about race. He repeatedly objected to the use of "Anglo Saxon," but Marcus was equally adamant that "English speaking" and "Spanish speaking" were not the way to describe the two sets of students. When documents giving the statistical breakdown of enrollment in the Garden Grove district were introduced and distinguished between "English speaking" and "non-English speaking" students, Marcus objected that they were misleading: "They are not accurate to this extent, your Honor, when they recite the fact that there are Spanish speaking pupils. . . . As a matter of fact, we are prepared to show that they speak English and spoke English prior to attending school. . . . Many of the parents, practically all of the parents in those particular districts, attended the schools that they are trying to get their children to go to now, and the parents are American citizens, most of them."

Holden, stating that he was merely attempting "to simplify a difficult situation," asked, "Don't we mean that it is people of Mexican descent who speak Spanish at home and in the communities where they reside?"

No, Marcus replied. "I am willing to say this, however, that they have the same proficiency with respect to speaking the English language as, we will say — what was the word your Honor suggested? I don't want to use the word Anglo Saxon."

THE COURT: English speaking people.
MR. MARCUS: You see, I run into that difficulty again, your Honor, because these children do speak English.

Holden denied that:

MR. HOLDEN: . . . When they come to school, they do not understand one word of English, that is, most of them don't. There are exceptions, and the petitioners in this case, I will admit the petitioners in this case, the named petitioners, probably are able to speak fairly good English, but they go into these schools, and they are not, in the lower grades, able to compete or to carry the work that the students who are familiar with the English language are able to do . . . [so] it would be an absolute necessity, if these children were all brought into the same school house, to put this group of Mexicans into one room or one class and the other pupils into another, because . . . they cannot advance together in the same grades.
THE COURT: Because of their linguistic difference?
MR. HOLDEN: Yes. Sure, they can speak some English, you know. They have to be able to understand a certain amount of English before they can go from one grade to another, but they cannot

grasp it. Where they have lived in the Spanish language, with Spanish customs, and they talk it at home, and as soon as they are out of school they go back to their homes and commence talking. So again, thinking in Spanish, they cannot compete with the other students and advance in the same grade at the same age. . . . There are so many of them in these particular districts that it is more advantageous, not only for the Mexicans, but for the teachers, for the administration of the school, to have them separated entirely.

McCormick was trying to be fair while he continued to wrestle with the question of nomenclature:

THE COURT: We are trying to classify them so as to accurately designate the various classifications, and not for any other purpose. A person may be of Spanish descent or origin, ancestry, and yet speak English perfectly as far as grammatical expression is concerned and as far as knowledge of the language is concerned, but yet they do have an accent. That is true in the United States. Native Americans reveal that. Those who are natives of one section of the country have certain peculiarities of speech and accent and inflection and pronunciation and idioms, that are not true of those born in another section of the United States. Yet they are born of English speaking parents and that has been their lineage for generations. So that that, I think, would not be a proper method of classifying the children that are involved in the question at issue before the Court.

MR. HOLDEN: . . . He designates them as Mexicans and of Mexican descent. We are all talking about the same people.

THE COURT: That's right; trying to, anyway.

Holden, too, found it difficult to decide whether race was an issue. Referring to the purported inability of the Mexican-American children to speak English, he said, "This is confusing me, too, because I don't want to say white people, because the Mexicans are white, but say the non-Mexican. In the first grade the Mexican, if he enters at five years old, he won't make the first grade the first year. The white pupil will easily advance to the first grade when he is six years old." At times, in the pretrial and trial proceedings, Mexican-Americans were spoken of as white; at others, they were distinguished from the white race. The artificiality of racial classifications could not have been starker.

Marcus, however, was firm in denying that the case involved race rather than ethnicity. He believed that Mexicans were white, and in any event, his case depended on denying that Supreme Court decisions such as *Plessy v. Ferguson* were relevant here. "We do not contend that there is such a thing as the Mexican race," he told the court. "That will eliminate the question of race. We do, however, contend that this adopted procedure of compulsory school attendance at these particular districts is based upon the fact that they are of Mexican or Latin descent."

THE COURT: There is no question of race.

MR. HOLDEN: No.

THE COURT: You don't contend that there is any question of race in the case, do you?

MR. MARCUS: No, there isn't, your Honor.

THE COURT: Of course not. So that those decisions [the Supreme Court precedents], I think, are not applicable at all. If we had a question of race, then it would present a different problem than we have. We have here a problem and the ultimate question would be what is meant by the same or equal facilities. That doesn't simply mean the curriculum. It means social, in the sense that children are in a democratic environment, commingling with one another on an equal basis as far as nature has constituted individuals to be equal. Of course, we must always have that in mind, that we are talking about practical questions from a practical point of view, and that we must take nature as we find it.

A child that is retarded mentally couldn't absorb the same facilities or grasp the same implements that a child that is normal could. Therefore, the school authorities not only have the right, but I presume it would be their duty, to segregate children in that way.

That is not the claim here, as I understand it. The claim here is that they have just taken the Mexican people, their children, en masse and drawn a line around where they live and said to them, "Now, you have to go to a school in this place here. You can't go to a school here where the others who aren't of this origin go."

McCormick's comment about the children "commingling with one another" may be seen, in retrospect, as a clue to the way he would come to feel about the segregation. His mind was not yet made up, however, and absent a clear showing of discrimination, he was not willing to say that the districts had acted illegally. If Marcus could not prove that the pupils sent to the "Mexican" schools were the linguistic equals of other children, "then there isn't much room to argue unjust discrimination, because I think it would have to be conceded that the Court couldn't set itself up as the standard of the school management except to ascertain whether because of some improper classification within the law the school authorities have arbitrarily and in a dictatorial manner used their own judgment in the segregation of people on account of language."

McCormick was not about to second-guess educators. At the same time, he read at length from the 1923 Supreme Court decision in the case of *Meyer v. Nebraska*. There, the Court held that a post–World War I state law forbidding the teaching of any language other than English was unconstitutional. As McCormick quoted the Court for the record, it ruled that although the state had great leeway over its educational system, " 'The protection of the Constitution extends to all, to those who speak other languages as well as to those born with English on the tongue. Perhaps it would be highly advantageous if all had ready understanding of our ordinary speech, but this cannot be coerced by methods which conflict with the Constitution—a desirable end cannot be promoted by prohibited means.' " The Court added, and again McCormick quoted, " 'It is well known that proficiency in a foreign language seldom comes to one not instructed at an early age, and experience shows that this is not injurious to the health, morals or understanding of the ordinary child.' " Whether that lack of proficiency justified the segregation here would have to be decided at trial.

Holden relied heavily on the fact that some "Spanish-speaking" children had been admitted to some of the other schools, and McCormick indicated that the evidence might show that there was therefore no discrimination on the basis of ethnicity. What, he asked rhetorically, was a "democratic method of public school instruction?" It seemed to him that if 30 percent of the pupils in a school were at grade level and others "failed to measure up scholastically to the requirements set forth by the school authorities," the 30 percent should not be held back by the others. He continued in a vein that could not have been reassuring to Marcus:

> The mere fact that a child, because of his lack of contact with or knowledge of a particular language may be handicapped in another – that is what the Supreme Court tried to say in this Nebraska case – doesn't show anything improper or doesn't show any reflection upon that child, any more than the placing of children who are of arrested mentality or who are lazy or who don't want to work in school in a room by themselves. That is no reflection on them, and it is within the proper scope of school authority. . . . The law requires that instruction in the public school system in California shall be in the English language. That means that children who cannot comprehend to the same degree instructions may be handicapped.

The case was a difficult one, McCormick said. "I don't believe there is any case in the books that parallels this case," although he thought the "principles" in *Meyer v. Nebraska* were "applicable" here. What exactly he found those principles to be he did not say.

McCormick asked whether the teachers in the "Mexican" schools were Spanish-speaking. "No, they are not," Holden replied, and he noted that there were a few "Spanish-speaking" students in the Westminster school and in a number of schools in Santa Ana. Marcus, whose emotions were being rubbed raw, objected that the Spanish-speaking students in the schools at issue had been sent letters saying they would no longer be welcome.

THE COURT: Was that because of scholarship attainments or restrictions?

MR. MARCUS: Because, as the letters indicate . . . there was objection from other students. . . .

THE COURT: You contend, then, that it was not because of scholarship attainment?

MR. MARCUS: Certainly not.

THE COURT: Don't get angry about it. I just asked you the question.

MR. MARCUS: It strikes home, your Honor.

Holden said that Westminster had agreed to desegregate six months before the *Mendez* case was filed. Marcus responded caustically: "They agreed to abandon that five or six years ago, but they didn't do it."

As McCormick summed up, the school districts admitted segregation but denied that it was based on discrimination. "Therefore," he admonished Marcus, "the question is: Is or is not the segregation an unjust discriminatory activity on the part of the school authorities? That is the thing to prove or disprove. You have got the burden of proof then."

"We have established the discrimination," Marcus objected.

"No," McCormick replied, "you have established segregation."

Holden reiterated that the courts had held that segregated education was constitutional as long as all students enjoyed equal facilities. Education, he insisted, was a state matter rather than one for the federal government or the federal courts, "and it is up to the state to determine whether they educate their people, and they can educate the girls and leave the boys out, and they can educate the people up to the age of 21, or they can start them to school at 10. That is not a matter of federal concern."

McCormick would decide whether the federal courts had jurisdiction only after hearing the plaintiffs' witnesses, he said. The case would go to trial.

CHAPTER 5

The Trial Begins

Manuela Ochoa was the first witness on the stand when the case of *Mendez v. Westminster* was called on Thursday, July 5, 1945, at 10 A.M. As she looked out at the courtroom, she could see David Marcus and three other lawyers for the plaintiffs. A. L. Wirin and J. B. Tietz were there, as amici, for the ACLU's Southern California branch. Charles F. Christopher was also on hand as amicus, representing the Los Angeles chapter of the National Lawyers Guild. Christopher would remain silent until the final day of the trial, when he would question a witness whose testimony would have a major impact on the outcome.

George Holden sat at the defendants' table with his boss, Joel Ogle, although Ogle would speak very little during the trial. At Marcus's request, Judge McCormick had granted permission for representatives of the Mexican consulates in Los Angeles and Santa Ana to sit in the space reserved for lawyers, "as a matter of courtesy to the Mexican government." Their presence reflected the Mexican government's interest in the case, but their lack of active participation suggested that the government preferred to maintain a low profile in what was essentially an internal American matter. Nonetheless, it appears that the Mexican government was quietly involved, for during the pretrial hearing, Marcus emphasized that both he and "the Mexican Government that I represent" had hoped the matter could be solved through negotiation rather than litigation.

Felícitas Méndez was in the courtroom, as were other members of the Mexican-American community. Parents from the Asociación de Padres de Niños México-Americanos that Felícitas had helped organize went to the trial every day to demonstrate support. Some of the laborers could not afford to give up the wages they lost due to their absence from work, so the Méndezes dug into their own pockets to reimburse them. All listened avidly as Marcus began to question Mrs. Ochoa.

Her testimony was typical of that given by parents in each of the four school districts over the next two weeks. The court agreed that the evidence would be presented district by district, and Mrs. Ochoa was there to speak about Garden Grove. She had been born in the United States, as had her four children, aged eight months to fourteen years. The three older children were bilingual, she said, although the family spoke English at home. In September 1944, some days before the school year began, she went to see Superintendent of Schools James L. Kent to ask that Rogelio Ochoa, then seven years old, be permitted to go to the Lincoln School. It was better than the Hoover School and closer to her home, she told Kent. Lincoln was only five blocks away, whereas Rogelio would have to be bused to Hoover. Nonetheless, Kent replied, her children could not attend Lincoln because, as she recalled his words, "children of Mexican ancestry were not admitted there."

Kent, who was then in his first year as Garden Grove superintendent, said he would double-check with the school board. He later went to Mrs. Ochoa's home to tell her that the answer was still no. She protested that some children of Mexican ancestry who lived closer to Hoover were nonetheless at Lincoln, and "he said they were probably from Spanish ancestry . . . if your children were registered as Spanish, they could attend the Lincoln School." "My children cannot be registered as Spanish, because their father is Mexican," she answered, so the child was sent to Hoover. The kind of treatment the children received there was reflected in Mrs. Ochoa's description of the school lunch: "They start with Monday and they cook the bone for the soup, or the meat, and they start from Monday until Friday with the same meat, and they just add vegetables and water to the same meat, and they boil it every day."

Rogelio had been present during the conversations, Mrs. Ochoa testified, but Kent neither spoke with him nor mentioned anything about language ability as a condition for going to Lincoln. "Who does go to Lincoln?" Marcus asked. "The white American children, and the Filipinos, and the Japanese and the Negroes," she responded. In fact, before California's Japanese-American population was sent to relocation camps, the Orange County school districts permitted Japanese-American children, whose parents had become tenant farmers rather than laborers, to attend the "white" schools. The same was true of other children of Asian ancestry, as well as African-American children. While the southern states were segregating students so as to shield white children from African-Americans, Orange County put whites and blacks together so as to shield them from Mexican-Americans.

Marcus followed up by entering into evidence statistics, supplied by the Garden Grove district, showing that all 349 children enrolled at Lincoln were listed as "English-speaking" and all 292 at Hoover as "Spanish-speaking." "There is segregation, of course," Judge McCormick acknowledged, but that wasn't what the case was about. "The case is discrimination, and segregation, in and of itself, doesn't indicate discrimination." The district kept Mexican-American children in the first grade for two years and in the second grade for two years, Marcus protested. "Suppose they do," McCormick commented. "If the school authorities think the child has not progressed, it is the duty of the school authorities to so indicate." The fact that they were considered slow learners did not prove discrimination, as opposed to a valid educational assessment, and so Marcus moved on to Frank Palomino, his next Garden Grove witness.

Marcus had to make two points successfully if he was going to win his case on the basis of the Fourteenth Amendment. His underlying argument, as we have seen, was that Mexican-American students were being denied the equal protection of the laws. Unlike the situation in the San Bernardino pool case, however, Mexican-Americans were not being denied facilities offered to other people. Nor was this similar to the higher education cases that had been won by the NAACP, for Marcus was not asserting that the facilities in the "Mexican" schools were inferior to those in the others. Marcus wanted to attack segregation itself, and to do so, he first had to demonstrate that the school districts were systemically segregating the students on the basis of ethnicity, without reference to their language or other academic abilities. That would knock out the districts' claim of language facility as the basis for the separation. As Mrs. Ochoa indicated, the children were given no tests before being assigned to "Mexican" schools.

Once he had made that point, Marcus could move on to his next challenge: showing that segregation resulted in the children's receiving an inferior education. Given the Supreme Court precedents, this was a radical claim: that "separate but equal" was not, in fact, equal.

Two of the main tasks of elementary schools were increasing language facility and enhancing integration into society. If the segregation was actually hurting the Mexican-American children's ability to improve their language skills and become both more knowledgeable about and more familiar with the larger society in which they lived — and if the students in the other schools were receiving such an education — then he could rightfully argue that they were being treated unequally. To make the second point, he would have to rely on experts. First, however, he had to show that all Mexican-American children, not just Mrs. Ochoa's child or some other child, were the objects of discrimination.

Marcus's purpose in calling Palomino was to demonstrate that the segregation of children in Garden Grove was a continuing pattern rather than an isolated phenomenon. Palomino recounted a conversation he had had in 1941 with Harvey Emley, Superintendent Kent's predecessor, similar to the one Mrs. Ochoa had with Kent three years later. Palomino too had been told that Mexican-American children could not attend Lincoln, and his children had not been tested for language proficiency. He placed one child in a parochial school rather than send him to Hoover. "Being in this country, as I am," Palomino told the court, "I want to live and I want to raise them as a good American, if they give us a chance." He was followed on the stand by Jane Sianez, whose three school-age children were forced to attend Hoover, although the family home was half a mile from the "white" Bolsa School and three miles away from Hoover. Again, no language test had been given to the children. The next witness was Juan Muñoz, whose conversation with Emley about children and dirt was recounted in chapter 3.

Marcus then called Superintendent Kent himself. In June 1941, before he became school superintendent of Garden Grove, Kent had submitted the thesis that earned him a master's degree in education from the University of Oregon and was mentioned in the early *Santa Ana Register* article about the *Mendez* case. It was entitled "Segregation of Mexican School Children in Southern California," and it argued that all "Mexican" students should be segregated. Kent referred throughout to "Mexicans," differentiating them from "Americans," and he made it clear that he believed Mexicans constituted a separate and nonwhite race. His first sentence was "Southern California is faced with a predominance of two races of people in its schools." Mexicans were "an alien race that should be segregated socially," and this had been accomplished in Southern California "by designating certain sections where they might live and restricting these sections to them" — in other words, keeping them out of "white" neighborhoods. "Upon investigation of the mental ability and moral characteristics of the average Mexican school child it is evident that this [housing segregation] is a condition which is advantageous to both the white and Mexican child. Segregation also into separate schools seems to be the ideal situation for both parties concerned." Because Mexican students could not be expected to keep up with their white classmates, segregation would be a "boon" to the Mexican children.

Unfortunately, Kent continued, Mexicans suffered from health problems. Foremost among these was malnutrition "due to their type of food," which consisted entirely of "tortillas, a greasy mixture, or enchiladas and beans." The number of communicable diseases contracted by Mexicans indicated that "the Mexican race is of a less sturdy stock than the white race." In addition, the "personal hygiene of the Mexican people is deplorable." All family members frequently used the same combs, towels, and washcloths. There was a high rate of infant mortality. The health problems were not surprising because, "as a general rule, most of the living is done in the back portion of the house, and this is usually a veritable junk heap — all pretense at cleanliness is here abandoned. . . . The few dishes they possess are usually dirty."

The families' "crowded living conditions . . . encourage rather than discourage loose morals." Morality was a key issue, according to Kent. "Children of Latin origins and background mature at an earlier age than those of an Anglo-Saxon or northern background and hence, are more subject to adult delinquencies than those of the white race." Kent appended Los Angeles police statistics demonstrating the high rate of juvenile arrests among Mexican-Americans to support his assertion. They routinely stole and cheated, in school as well as outside it. Worse still, "educational standards are very low among the Mexican people." Citing students who had dropped out of school to help their families, he deplored the large number of children produced by each family and made it clear that family values were not one of his priorities — at least not for Mexican-Americans. "The Mexican attitude toward education seems to be one of indifference. The cause of the family comes first regardless of the benefits of education." When this "attitude" was coupled with "their racial language handicap" and IQ differences between the two "races," it became clear that "a separate curriculum adjusted to them is advisable . . . a curriculum based upon their abilities . . . would probably help solve the problem of assisting the Mexican in becoming a worthwhile citizen." The segregation of such students should be "complete" and should include "separate plots of ground, separate buildings and separate teachers." Kent nonetheless denied that his advocacy of segregation suggested that Mexicans were "unwanted people," because "economically they have been beneficial to southern California." So they could stay as long as they stayed in their place — which was away from "white" schools and in low-paying jobs.

These were the views of the man charged with educating the children of Garden Grove. His wholesale condemnation of the Mexican "race" was breathtaking enough. What made it even more so were the authorities cited and quoted by Kent. They included articles from an array of scholarly journals in sociology and psychology, as well as books published by university presses. Anyone reading his thesis might well believe that leading American scholars viewed Mexican-Americans as belonging to a biologically inferior race that should be kept apart from whites for the good of all concerned.

Marcus had read the thesis, and it was now his job to show the court that Kent's views, as they were applied in Garden Grove, were based on racism rather than on legitimate pedagogic considerations. Marcus asked Kent whether it was Garden Grove policy to send "children of Mexican descent" to Hoover. No, Kent replied, but "the policy does read that for non-English-speaking students and students who need help, we have set up the Hoover School for the Spanish-speaking students." The "Spanish-speaking students" were those "who come to school with a language handicap. Not necessarily that they speak Spanish all the time, but that they have a bilingual handicap" and therefore had to be placed in special classes. Interestingly, according to Kent's testimony, Japanese and Filipino children did not share that handicap, nor did the Portuguese or the "Negroes" in the district, none of whom was sent to Hoover. When asked whether all the children at Hoover had language problems, Kent said that this was not the case, but because the non–bilingually handicapped Mexican-American children lived right near Hoover, "it would be silly to transport them to any other school."

Another reason for the "absolute segregation," to which Kent readily admitted, was "social behavior." Marcus asked, "What do you mean by that?"

A [KENT]: We mean that Mexican children have to be American-ized much more highly than our so-called American children. . . . They must be taught cleanliness, and they must be taught manners, which ordinarily do not come out of the home . . . the cleanliness of mind, mannerisms, dress, ability to get along with other people.

Q [MARCUS]: And you find that Mexican children that attend school between the first and sixth grades require all that? . . . without any special tests or examinations, that applies to the entire Mexican children of Mexican descent; is that correct?

A: Oh, no. We give tests.

Q: But you are giving these special classes or courses in this Hoover School, are you?

A: All schools.

Q: All schools?

A: Yes, sir.

Q: But why are you segregating, then, the Mexican children, if you are giving them to all of them?

A: Because we feel we can do a better job with our Mexican chil-dren where we have trained teachers to care for them.

Marcus would return to the question of language tests and the training of teachers later. For the moment, he pushed Kent on the issue of why no Mexican-American children were permitted to trans-fer out of Hoover.

Q: If a child speaks English, and is clean, and lives near the other school besides the Hoover School, does that make any differ-ence?

A: It would make a difference, then.

Q: Would you expect him to go to the Lincoln School?

A: All things being equal, we would . . .

Q: Do you have now at least one Mexican child attending the Lin-coln School?

A: No, sir.

George Holden then cross-examined Kent about Mexican-American children's knowledge of English when they first enrolled in school. "We usually find them retarded," Kent answered, meaning that they were unable to work at grade level. The "retarded" children were "in a pre-primer class, which we set up primarily to teach them reading readily. It usually puts them one year behind." Of the children who came to school speaking English, Kent stated, "the large percentage of them can speak the English language, or they can understand it, but that does not necessarily mean that they can progress in school . . . by our tests we find that they are a year retarded in comparison with the white children."

"Let's not refer to the children as white," Holden interjected.

On redirect examination, Marcus pushed harder:

Q: Did I understand you to say, Mr. Kent, that it was for the benefit of the Mexican children that they were being segregated?
A: That's right.
Q: And that was because they were retarded about one year in their knowledge of the courses they were given in the respective grades, is that right? . . . Now, is it a fact, then, that all children of Mexican extraction, to your mind, are retarded?
A: No.
Q: Are there some that are not retarded?
A: Yes.
Q: Are any of those "some" that you referred to permitted to go to the other school?
A: No . . . but they are not placed in the beginning group.

What happened to "children other than those of Mexican descent that retard" the Lincoln School or the Bolsa School? Marcus wondered.

A: We have special work with them.
Q: In what way? What special work have you?
A: Sometimes we keep them after hours and the teachers work with them, or she has small reading groups and works with them.
Q: Couldn't that be done as well with the Mexican children?

A: No . . . it couldn't, because our teachers would not be trained to work with the Mexican children.

The question of the special training given to Hoover teachers had to be explored.

Q: What particular training do they have?
A: Experience over a period of years.
Q: Experience over a period of years at the Hoover School? . . .
A: That is where they got their experience.
Q: That is where, because of the segregation, they got their experience?
A: That's right.

In other words, there was no special training of the teachers. Marcus was losing patience.

Q: Let's get right down to brass tacks. This school [Hoover] was built for the Mexican children; is that correct?
A: Yes, sir.
Q: And it was built there for them regardless of their ability to speak the English language?
A: It was built to help them.
Q: Regardless of their ability to speak the English language; is that right?
A: That's right.

Kent had inadvertently admitted that language was not the sole criterion for segregating students, and Marcus followed up on that point. The attorney read from the Garden Grove school district's answer to the complaint, which had been signed by Kent, averring that "a large percentage of said persons [the Mexican-American students] residing in said communities have not been instructed in or are familiar with the proper rules of personal hygiene."

Q: Is that one of your reasons for this segregation at the Hoover School?

A: Yes, sir.

Q: Please tell the court in what particular of personal hygiene, that you have knowledge of, these children are not acquainted?

A: In the care of their heads, lice, impetigo, tuberculosis; generally dirty hands, face, neck, ears.

Q: Are all the children dirty?

A: No, sir.

Q: Or affected with lice, impetigo and tuberculosis?

A: No.

Q: How many of them?

A: I don't know. I would have to get our health figures to give you that. A large portion.

Marcus decided to tackle Kent's beliefs, as expressed in his thesis.

Q: Is it not a fact that you believe that the Mexican is not of the white race?

A: I believe he is an American. I don't believe he is of the white race, no.

The court then took a short recess. When it resumed, Marcus pursued the race question.

Q: . . . Mr. Kent, with respect to educational ability, it is your opinion that the Mexican children are inferior to the white children?

A: In their ability, yes.

Q: . . . What percentage of children of Mexican descent are inferior to the other children? . . .

A: 75 per cent.

Q: Now, in what other respects are the children of Mexican descent inferior to the other children in your district?

A: In their economic outlook, in their clothing, their ability to take part in the activities in school.

Q: . . . when you refer to the Mexican children, you refer to them as other than those of the Caucasian race?

A: No.

Q: You include them in the Caucasian race?

A: Yes, I was merely talking as to color when I said white.

Q: Well, then, at this time you believe that a Mexican is of the Caucasian race?

A: Yes.

Q: And is of the white race?

A: Yes.

Q: When did you determine that, during the recess?

A: No.

THE COURT: Now, I don't want any of that.

Judge McCormick wanted more information about the reasons for the segregation. He asked Kent whether there were Mexican-American students in Garden Grove who had moved from other California school districts. Kent replied that there were, but that a child who came with fourth-grade credentials from another district "might not be a fourth-grade student in our school." McCormick queried further, "Why can't you try him in one of the schools where you get what we might call a conglomeration of children?" Kent's answer was that Mexican-American children new to the district usually moved to the Hoover area. As the judge continued his questioning, Kent's change of heart about racial categories became shaky.

THE COURT: Do you mean by that, Mr. Kent, that those children who might be readily assimilable in the school where the generally democratic school population exists, such as in the Lincoln School . . . that the only reason [they] are not permitted to go to the Lincoln School is because they reside within a district that the school authorities have fixed as the district of the Hoover or the Bolsa School?

A: That is one of the reasons, but not all of them, I would say, Judge, because there is a psychology of the thing. There is one thing in putting one lone Mexican child in a group of 40 white children merely because he has come up to the level of the other white children, which is not fair to him, and we haven't done that . . . to put him in a whole class of white people, and put him in there by himself, would not be fair to him or to the other children.

McCormick wondered why children who were not up to grade level couldn't be put in a separate room in an integrated school, "where the children have the opportunity of mixing socially in a democratic way on the playground." Kent responded that the other schools were already overcrowded, and getting students from the Hoover area to those schools would present transportation problems. Later in the day, McCormick asked whether there was a playground in Garden Grove where "the children of all types" could play together. Kent said that the students in the high school, which was integrated, segregated themselves. His answer reflected a belief that Mexican-Americans were biologically distinct: "They will speak Spanish on the school grounds, and the white child simply doesn't understand, and, naturally, he isn't going to get in with them. Your Mexican child is advanced, that is, he matures physically faster than your white child, and he is able to do more in games. Therefore, he goes more on physical prowess than he does on mental ability."

After Superintendent Kent was excused, Marcus turned to the situation in Santa Ana. That district had fourteen elementary schools, and the ones at issue in the litigation were Delhi, Fremont, Logan, and Franklin. As of March 1945, Franklin had 237 students, of whom 161 were listed by the school as English-speaking and 76 as Spanish-speaking. Felícitas Fuentes, the mother of eight-year-old Roberto, was called to the witness stand. Mrs. Fuentes initially enrolled Roberto in Franklin's kindergarten. He had been there for one week when his teacher brought him to the Fuentes home and said that although he was bright, his English was good, and she wanted him in the class, Mrs. Fuentes would have to get permission from the assistant superintendent if Roberto was to stay. Otherwise, even though the family lived only one and a half blocks away from Franklin, he would have to go to the "Mexican" Fremont School. Mrs. Fuentes spoke with Assistant Superintendent Robert H. Reinhard and was so appalled at being denied permission for the transfer that she kept Roberto out of school for two years. Each September, from 1942 through 1944, she tried to get Roberto into Franklin. When he turned eight, the age specified in California's compulsory education law, she had no choice but to send him to Fremont.

Joe, the oldest Fuentes son, was in the U.S. Navy, stationed in the Philippines. The impact of the experience of war service on the Mexican-American community was apparent in some of Mrs. Fuentes's comments. In one of their conversations, Reinhard had asked her why the Mexican people were so dirty. "I told him that if our Mexican people were dirty, and all that, why didn't they have all of our boys that are fighting overseas, and all that, why didn't they bring them back and let us have them home . . . I told him if Joe wasn't qualified, why didn't they let me have him and not take him overseas, as he is right now."

Holden, cross-examining Fuentes, asked if she knew that Franklin was a "very much smaller" school than Fremont. She answered, "Yes, maybe it is, but if it is big enough for some other children to go there, I think it is big enough for my child, and for the children that are claiming their rights . . . why don't they divide and have all the children, the Mexican descent and the American citizens, have the same rights and teach them just the same, and mingle with the Americans right along with the citizens of the United States, as I am."

Fuentes had asked Reinhard if he would send a child of his own to Fremont: "And he told me, 'No.' I asked him, 'Why?' And he said, 'Because they don't have any privileges, and that I would want the best for my child.' I said, 'If you want the best for your child, I want the best for mine, too.'"

When the trial resumed on Friday, July 6, William Guzmán, the man who had hired attorney Charles Martin to represent him before the school board when his English-speaking child was kept out of Franklin, told much the same story as the parents who had already testified. So did Mabel Méndez. Two of her five children, now ten and thirteen years old, had attended Franklin, and she had gone to its PTA meetings regularly. When she received the October 1944 letter saying that the children would have to attend the Fremont School in the future, she and what she remembered as about twenty-five other Mexican parents went to a meeting of the school board. That was the meeting to which Guzmán took attorney Martin, and at which the board had said it would consider the matter. Judge McCormick asked why she did not want her children to attend Fremont. She responded:

Knowing they don't progress very much at the Fremont, I didn't want him to go back on his grades. . . . I had neighbors there that lived for quite a while there, and their children were just as old as mine, and they seemed like they didn't get anywhere, and quite a few of them that I have known, they haven't been very far ahead, at the Fremont, like they have at the Franklin. . . . I have one boy [who had gone to Franklin] that . . . graduated from Willard [the junior high school] at the age of 16, and my little neighbor [who went to Fremont] was 16 years of age and . . . hadn't graduated from the fifth grade.

As he had when presenting the Garden Grove evidence, Marcus called the superintendent of schools to the stand. Frank Henderson agreed that all the children at the Fremont and Delhi schools were Mexican-Americans and that the approximately thirty-five white children in the Fremont district and the approximately five in the Delhi district had been given special permission to attend another school. It was "the custom of these other children to get oral permission," he explained, and Mexican-American parents could request such permission as well. He admitted, however, that the Guzmáns and other parents who had asked for such permission during the school board meeting had received no answer. The African-American children in the Fremont district all went to other schools, and Judge McCormick wanted to know why. The answer suggested the way in which racial categorizations were foremost in the district's thinking:

A [HENDERSON]: The little colored children who reside in the Fremont district are very few. I think somebody said here four in one neighborhood. They are permitted to transfer to the school — as they are in a very small minority, they are permitted to transfer to the school where they will find the most of their own people. . . .

Q [MCCORMICK]: . . . Does that mean that the transfer in such cases is made automatically, without a request coming from the parents or guardians of those children?

A: Practically so, I think, your Honor.

Marcus followed up:

Q: Mr. Henderson, you have testified that it is the settled policy of the Santa Ana School Board, and yourself, that whenever any group, such as those of Mexican descent, are in the minority in a school district, that you permit those of that group to transfer to a school in another district wherein they would constitute a majority. Am I correct in that assumption?

A: You are right; Mexicans and others, too.

Q: That is right. If those who were not of Mexican descent were in a minority in a school district, would you permit them to transfer out to a school where they would be in the majority?

A: Yes, we do so.

Asked whether "the policy is to keep together, to constitute a majority, all members of a certain group of person, such as Mexicans, or others," Henderson nonetheless said that no such policy existed. "It is not a policy," Henderson said. "It is a permissive," based on requests from parents. Judge McCormick found that a bit confusing.

THE COURT: I don't quite understand, Mr. Henderson, the theory of the policy of the Board of Education in attempting to classify the student body in public schools according to a majority or minority basis.

THE WITNESS [HENDERSON]: Well, may I again explain concerning the colored children. Here are four colored children who were in the Fremont district and entered the Fremont School where they lived. The principal, who is here, said to them, "Now, you may stay here, if you like, but the majority of your kind, of the Negroes, are in the Franklin School. Therefore, you may transfer to the Franklin School where you will not be the only colored children, if you wish." Is that an explanation?

THE COURT: I understand that. Now, suppose instead of being the Negro children, it was the Mexican children. Would the same privilege be extended to them? . . . Would the overture come from the school authorities, as you stated it would to the Negroes?

THE WITNESS: No.

THE COURT: Why would there be any difference?

THE WITNESS: Well, partly through ignorance. Now, these Negroes didn't know anything about that privilege partly, I think, through ignorance. As I explained this morning, there are a good many Mexican children who live and could attend school in the Franklin District, where they are in a minority, who prefer to go to the Fremont School, which is purely Mexican and they are privileged to do so because they would be a minority, and they go into the school where it is 100 per cent Mexican.

Judge McCormick asked Henderson whether all the children at Fremont were "so-called Mexican children" and whether there were other Santa Ana schools "wherein all of the pupils are of the Caucasian race." Yes, Henderson replied; three schools had no Mexican-American pupils, and a fourth had only one. The confusion about how to typify children by race surfaced once again.

THE COURT: In that classification you have employed the term "Caucasian" in what manner?

THE WITNESS [HENDERSON]: Other than Mexican.

THE COURT: I didn't mean it that way. I meant "Caucasian" as all of those pupils who are not Mongolian or African.

THE WITNESS: Well, of course, Mexicans are Caucasians, aren't they?

THE COURT: I think so. I have always considered them so.

THE WITNESS: Yes.

THE COURT: Of course, I don't pretend to be an ethnologist or anthropologist.

Marcus asked how the school district determined which children were Mexican-American. By their names, Henderson replied.

The next school district to be discussed was El Modena, and Marcus began that presentation by calling fourteen-year-old Carol Torres. As recounted in chapter 3, she and her classmates had had a conversation with their principal about why only Mexican-Americans went to Lincoln. She spoke English before she began school, but she and all five of her school-age siblings had gone to or were attending Lincoln. She described Lincoln as separated from Roosevelt only by baseball diamonds. Lincoln began its school day at 8:20, she thought; Roosevelt, at 9:45. (It would become clear that these times were incorrect but that the schools did begin at different hours.) The two schools had recess at different times, so except for the competitive games organized by the schools, the children did not mix. That was verified by seventeen-year-old Robert Pérez, the next witness, who had also graduated from Lincoln. Lorenzo Ramirez, the father who had told Superintendent Harold Hammarsten that he thought people of different backgrounds would mix together freely one day, summarized that conversation. It was then time for Hammarsten to testify.

If Marcus was to prove that the districts had conspired to segregate and discriminate against Mexican-American students, he had to show that the districts were in contact. The first thing he elicited from Hammarsten was that the superintendents of the Orange County school districts met roughly once a month. Hammarsten added that it was policy in El Modena to separate Mexican-American children and that the policy had been in existence when he became superintendent seven years earlier. It was his understanding that the policy was around fifteen years old—something else Marcus had to get into the record to show that there was a continuing pattern of discrimination rather than a few separate acts. Hammarsten first confirmed the two students' testimony about Lincoln and Roosevelt having different opening hours—Lincoln, 8:30, and Roosevelt, 8:45—and recess times, but he added that grades one through three had recess and dismissal from school at the same time. The children nonetheless played separately, and Marcus did not follow up on the issue of to what extent that was voluntary.

Hammarsten believed that it was in the best interests of both English-speaking and non-English-speaking students to be educated separately. No language test was given before children were assigned to Lincoln, he acknowledged, and then he made the rather remarkable statement that "it is highly impossible to test a child that can't speak the English language," and "there is no reason to give them a test." Asked about Carol Torres, who had demonstrated that she spoke English well, Hammarsten replied that she "is one of our best students. . . . She has an I.Q. that is very high." Marcus asked if she had ever been told that she could ask to transfer to Roosevelt. "I don't think it was necessary," Hammarsten responded, admitting that he had never of his own volition transferred a child with special aptitude and sufficient English from Lincoln to Roosevelt. That would accomplish nothing, he maintained, because "if we put all the Mexican children and the children of the Roosevelt School together and classified them according to ability in the first grade, it would naturally throw all of the Mexican students into one group." Throughout the trial, all the superintendents insisted that for pedagogic reasons, "Mexican" children would have to be kept in separate classes even if they were physically located in the same school building as other children. At the same time, Hammarsten acknowledged that there were children such as Torres who were intelligent and capable of doing sophisticated work. In fact, he said, the most recent seventh grade at the Lincoln School had performed well above the norm. That impelled Judge McCormick to step in.

THE COURT: Is it true, Mr. Hammarsten, that what you call the level of the Lincoln School . . . you consider to be different than the level of the Roosevelt School . . . ?

A: . . . According to standardized tests that we give, the children in the Lincoln School do not come up to the same level that the children in the Roosevelt School do, with one exception. We have a seventh grade in the Lincoln School that is comprised of students that have a higher mental ability, and as a result they are above the standard norm.

Q: . . . Well, let us take that seventh grade class in the Lincoln School last year. You say that was an unusually efficient class?

A: Yes. . . .

Q: I suppose, notwithstanding that fine degree of efficiency that the class maintained, that there were in that class certain pupils who were outstanding in the class?

A: Oh, surely.

Q: Why couldn't they be transferred into the Roosevelt School?

A: Well, they could, if we had room to accept them in there, for one thing, and on the other hand, the children themselves or their parents have never made application to come there, and most of the children, from my being with them all the time there, I gather they are completely satisfied with their present status. . . .

Q: Why isn't it practicable . . . for the school authorities to assign children without regard to their ancestry, but with respect to their intellectual attainment and scholarship classification? . . . Then isn't it possible . . . to segregate the children according to their mental and intellectual ability?

A: It is possible, certainly.

Q: But that hasn't been done, has it?

It was better to keep the Mexican-American children together, Hammarsten said, because that way, the smarter ones could assume leadership roles that otherwise would have been impossible. He continued:

> The advantage to this system is that the children that are high mentally amongst the Mexican group become the leaders in that group and form the nucleus, from the whole educational standpoint. They are the leaders. They are the ones that push the program in that classroom, and it is a distinct advantage to have those children in the Mexican school. And it is better for them, because it gives them the opportunity to display leadership . . . the better students are always selected as class representatives, to Student Body Councils, and they are the ones that are given the opportunity to speak at their grade exercises. . . . If you took those out of the Mexican school, it would leave the lower class again by themselves, and there would be no initiative for those that are left . . . they need the aggressiveness of those of the higher type to push the activity in the classroom and in school activities.

Court adjourned until the following Monday, with Marcus promising to conclude his case in no more than an hour and a half. Holden was certain that he could present the defendants' case in a day. When the trial resumed, it would focus on the Westminster school district, and it would go on for longer than Marcus anticipated.

CHAPTER 6

"We Always Tell Our Children They Are Americans"

David Marcus went into court on Monday, July 9, at a distinct disadvantage. He was apparently staying in Los Angeles rather than returning home to Pasadena every night, and his car had been stolen over the weekend. The suitcase with his clothes was in the car. Worse yet, so was the briefcase with all his papers for the case. Nonetheless, he was able to begin the day by putting Richard F. Harris, the Westminster superintendent of schools for the last two years, on the witness stand.

By the time of the trial, Westminster claimed that it was already in the process of desegregating and so should not be a party to the suit. Its plan, Harris said, was to move the all–Mexican-American Hoover School's buildings to the all-Anglo Westminster school. The decision had been made at a school board meeting on September 19, 1944, and reiterated at another meeting on January 16, 1945. At the January meeting, according to the minutes quoted in chapter 3 and at trial by Marcus, "Mr. Mendez was informed that the idea of placing all children in one school was not a new topic of the Board and that they had given it serious consideration in October, 1943." The minutes indicated that the board had also told Méndez that the move could not take place in 1944 because of insufficient funds. In court, Harris said that bids for work on the Westminster school had gone out on July 6, 1945. Why bids had not been obtained in 1944 was unclear—unless, of course, it had taken the threat of litigation to get the board to act. "It appears the costs are prohibitive," Harris now lamented. It was clear to Marcus that no such move would take place in the absence of a court order.

Forty percent of the Mexican-American children entering first grade in Westminster's Hoover School could not speak English, Harris testified, and the other 60 percent spoke English but "were below the part of the first grade group at the Westminster School." In addition, once the children's English improved, they still "do not progress along as the others [at the Westminster school], due to the fact perhaps of their cultural background or language heritage," and they lacked "American culture as seen through English words."

> Q [MARCUS]: What distinction do you find amongst these children in their cultural development, whether they speak the English language or they don't speak the English language?
>
> A [HARRIS]: In an English-speaking home, English language, there are certain cultural backgrounds which undoubtedly were formed, many of them, and came in earlier days from England. Out of those come Mother Goose rhymes. Out of those come stories. Out of those come stories of our American heroes, stories of our American frontier, rhymes, rhythms. Now, let us compare the cultural background which the child of Mexican-speaking families come[s] to us with. He apparently has not had these stories read to him in the English language. He has no conception of them, and the fact of the matter is that as to certain objects, he doesn't know their meaning in English. He knows them in Spanish. He has no conception of them when you put the word in English.

Judge McCormick asked whether the Mexican-American children of parents born and educated in the United States, having imbibed American culture, would not be better off in Westminster. No, Harris replied, because the children's language and cultural deficiencies meant they would still have to be in separate groups and separate rooms. Marcus pressed Harris on that point, and Harris appeared to contradict himself about the beneficial effects of "English" culture.

> Q: Is it your opinion, Mr. Harris, that children of Mexican descent are inferior because of their lack of English cultural background?
>
> A: Definitely not. They are inferior only in so far as their ability to grasp English words and meanings and conceptions are concerned.

Later in the day, however, he reverted to his assertion that descent was crucial and implied that he conflated a Mexican heritage with a lack of proficiency in speaking English. In referring to the 60 percent of students he acknowledged could speak English, "It is the degree of sufficiency which they have acquired in the understanding and use and conception of symbols and words of the English language, which is still not up to the children of Anglo-Saxon descent," he explained. "I think this retardation of children who enter from homes who speak the Spanish language in their homes," he went on, "well, I think that the retardation continues. I would say that there is a degree to which it handicaps the child." Children in the third grade at Hoover still did not have "efficiency in the English language," which he defined as "being able to carry on a conversation in the English language, to be responsive to certain questions in a clear and in a larger answer than 'Yes' or 'No.'" Perhaps only 5 percent of the children in the fourth, fifth, and sixth grades had that efficiency; perhaps 10 to 12 percent of those in the eighth grade had it. He did not explain why those 10 to 12 percent were not transferred to Westminster. Asked about Méndez's request to have his children attend Westminster, Harris replied, "His request was never rejected." The only reason the children were not transferred was that Westminster was overcrowded; the Méndez children would be allowed to go there "in so far as when conditions of housing were available."

If Harris and the school board really believed the insistent justification for separate schools that Harris presented to the court, it was not clear why the district had moved in the direction of desegregation at all. If their motives were purely pedagogical, keeping the children separated made sense. Now that the board had voted in principle to combine the schools, Marcus asked, did Harris think that was a good thing? It was a clear invitation for Harris to contradict himself, alienating his school board employers no matter what position he took, and he declined to do so.

Q: Is it your opinion that it is beneficial now to the children of the Hoover School to permit them to associate with, and attend at other schools in the district, without segregation?

A: Since that hasn't been done, I have no information leading to that belief either way.

Q: Well, you, as an educator and superintendent of schools, can give us your opinion, could you not?

A: One's opinion oft times is of such a small consequence.

Like Hammarsten, and perhaps because he had heard Hammarsten's testimony, Harris also argued that segregation gave Mexican-American students a chance to exercise leadership.

Gonzalo Méndez took the stand when Harris was finished. He testified that at the school board meeting of September 6, 1944, one board member had suggested that all the students currently enrolled in the two schools could be kept where they were, but all incoming children could be put into Main. Méndez had objected because that would keep his younger son, seven-year-old Gerónimo, who had just begun school, in a segregated school through eight grades.

Court then recessed, and when it reconvened the following day, July 10, Méndez took the stand once again. Judge McCormick asked him whether his wife spoke English, and the colloquy that followed reflected the jurist's attempt to grapple with a situation that was clearly new to him.

A [MÉNDEZ]: She speaks English a little like me, with a little broken accent or dialect, you might call it.

Q [MCCORMICK]: Well, of course, that would be natural. That would apply not only to the Mexican people. Any person of Latin or Slavic or Teutonic origin, or perhaps of other origin, would naturally have some. It might be an accent or a brogue. It might be even in our own country where some one would have an accent because he comes from the south or from New England. It is readily ascertainable. I don't mean the accent. I mean the ability to express one's thoughts in words in the English language.

A: She can carry on a good conversation in English. . . .

Q: Well, did you and she have any difficulty in understanding each other in what you call your Mexican language and what she would call her Spanish?

A: No, your Honor. We have no difficulty, although she claims that they talk a better Spanish in her country than my country, but it is all the same Spanish.

Q: You mean it is fundamentally and basically a derivation of the Spanish language?

A: Yes.

Felícitas Méndez was called next. Marcus asked her about the school board meeting. "We got kind of sore, especially me," she replied. "We always tell our children they are Americans, and I feel I am American myself, and so is my husband, and we thought that they shouldn't be segregated like that, they shouldn't be treated the way they are. So we thought we were doing the right thing and just asking for the right thing, to put our children together with the rest of the children there."

Holden interrupted to say that he was willing, in the interest of time, to stipulate that she would verify what her husband had said. Marcus responded that he would accept the stipulation, but added, "I thought the court and counsel would like to hear her converse in the English language." McCormick was satisfied that she could do so: "She seems to have a pretty good knowledge of the vernacular, beyond the commonplace vernacular, and as it should be spoken." Marcus had her testify that the children also spoke English, and she was excused.

Marcus's last witness was John Marval, a Santa Ana resident and small-business man. Marval's mother was Puerto Rican and his father, born in Venezuela, was half Spanish and half French. That was enough to make him and his children "of Latin descent" in the eyes of the Santa Ana school board. Marval had attended the Franklin School in Santa Ana back in the 1920s, before it was so rigidly segregated, and he tried to enroll his oldest child there. The principal of Franklin sent him to Winton Smith, the director of child welfare and attendance of the Santa Ana schools. Smith pulled out a map and told Marval, "You are in the Mexican district, and you have to send your child to the Fremont School."

"I will send him to the Fremont School with this condition," Marval responded: "that you send all your white children from the white families to the Fremont School."

That could not be done, Smith told him, "because there are fewer white children in that district, and we naturally have to bring them across to the Franklin School."

When Marval said he absolutely would not send his children to

Fremont, Smith answered that Marval would go to jail. Marval recounted more of the conversation:

> I said, "I will rot in jail before I see my child go back to that school." I says, "I own property here in Santa Ana, and I have got a business here, and I don't see why my child can't have the same opportunity the rest of them have."
>
> And he says, "The trouble with you Mexican folks, or the Mexican people," he says, "you are dirty." He says, "You know that a lot of Mexicans have their—they got bugs in their hair, and are not too clean behind their ears."
>
> And I got kind of mad. I said, "Well, Mr. Smith I have got my boy right here, and you see how dirty his ears are and how many bugs he has in his hair."
>
> So he says, "Mr. Marval, that is a little different. I wasn't saying that just for you, I am saying that for a group."
>
> I said, "I am fighting for my child. I don't care how other people dress, or are, but I want him to learn so that he won't be ashamed to be here either."
>
> With that he says, "There is nothing that can be done about it."
>
> I says, "All right. I am going to see my lawyer and see if I could get my child in there or not."
>
> He said, "You can do whatever you do, but he won't go to the Franklin School."
>
> I says, "He is going to go to Franklin School."

Marval immediately went to see his attorney, Charles Martin, who called Henderson. Henderson in turn went to the school board, who decided to admit Marval's son Johnny "as a special privilege." Henderson would testify the next day that Johnny was allowed to transfer because he was "not of Mexican descent." Marval nonetheless received the October 1944 form letter from Yost saying that his son would be sent back to Fremont the following year.

When the plaintiffs rested, Holden asked the court to dismiss the case. The court had no jurisdiction, he claimed, because there had been no deprivation of civil rights, and no proof of a conspiracy had been offered. More to the point, he argued, the school boards had not acted "in an arbitrary or dictatorial manner." On the contrary, "the evidence in this case shows, in my opinion, and demonstrates, in my opinion, the operation of democracy, American democracy, as it is practiced in that level of the government which is closest to the people."

Holden's view of what had happened was quite different from that of the plaintiffs. "Take the Westminster case," for example, he said. "There Mr. Mendez felt that he was aggrieved by segregation, and . . . it has been going on for some years, and . . . the first word that ever got to the Board of Trustees of Westminster was when Mr. Mendez decided to make a complaint. He went to the County Superintendent of Schools in Santa Ana and, as he testified, he was treated very courteously." He then went to Harris, who sent him to the school board. "That is the American way of doing it." When he went to the board, "it was a very friendly conversation." A few days later the board adopted a resolution to combine the schools, finances permitting. "There is the plain democratic way in which democracy operates," Holden observed. There was certainly no discrimination in Santa Ana, because "the evidence is that they permit some Negroes and some others than Negroes and some of the Mexican race to go to other schools outside that district upon special permit." In fact, Santa Ana had had separate schools for fifteen years, and no one had ever complained before the suit was filed. Similarly, Garden Grove's policy was fifteen or twenty years old, and not a single person had objected until Mrs. Ochoa made her complaint. In short, the school districts had exercised their powers in an appropriate manner, they had heard no objections from the communities involved, and when the plaintiffs did complain, appropriate and fair processes were followed. "This case certainly represents democracy," Holden declared once more, "operating as democracy should."

Judge McCormick did not accept Holden's invitation to discuss the nature of democracy. "Of course, we haven't here any question of race discrimination," he began instead. Both sides had agreed to that—Marcus because of the Supreme Court's decisions upholding the constitutionality of racial discrimination, and Holden because the school districts' defense was that the segregation was based on language ability and therefore not discriminatory. But because this was not a race case, McCormick stated, there were no precedents directly on point. He turned to *Kerr et al. v. Enoch Pratt Free Library of Baltimore City*, a 1944 case brought after the Board of Library Trustees of the City of

Baltimore refused to permit an African-American woman to take a qualifying examination for library service. The federal trial court held that there was no violation of the Fourteenth Amendment, which applies only to the states ("No *state* shall deny to any person within its jurisdiction the equal protection of the laws"), because the library corporation was a private rather than a state agency. The court of appeals based its 1945 reversal of the trial court's holding in part on the precedent of *Nixon v. Condon* (1932), in which the Supreme Court had ruled that the executive committee of a Texas political party, authorized by Texas law to determine party members' qualifications, was a state entity. That, McCormick said, was analogous, because school districts are "instrumentalities of the State." Because the question of whether the districts' actions violated the Fourteenth Amendment was a valid one and was based on the U.S. Constitution, the federal courts did have jurisdiction. Holden's motion to dismiss was denied. The court broke for lunch, and the defense would have to present its case once court resumed in the afternoon.

At 2:00 Holden was ready to call James L. Kent, superintendent of the Garden Grove school district. Before he did so, Marcus received the court's permission to introduce into evidence Kent's master's thesis, which the plaintiffs believed demonstrated Kent's convictions about the inferiority of Mexican-Americans. Holden ignored the thesis and instead questioned Kent about his conversation with Mrs. Ochoa. "Did you have any conversation with the child?" Holden asked, referring to Rogelio Ochoa.

A: No.
Q: Did you say anything to the child?
A: Yes.
Q: And what did you say?
A: I tried to say, "Hello."
Q: Tried to say, "Hello"?
A: And to get the child in conversation.
Q: And what did the child say?
A: I didn't have any response.

Kent apparently believed that this demonstrated the seven-year-old's inability to speak English. His belief was reinforced by his visit to the Ochoa home, where, he testified, he heard Mrs. Ochoa talking with her other children in Spanish. That was bad because a child from a Spanish-speaking home "would definitely be handicapped throughout his school life." Judge McCormick asked whether "this bilingual handicap," as Kent called it, would not be diminished as the child progressed in school. That depended on what the child did outside of school, Kent replied. The school day was only four hours long. If the child persisted in speaking Spanish the rest of the day, there was little the school could do. Wouldn't the child be helped by being placed with others who spoke English? McCormick wondered. No, Kent said, because the child had other "inefficiencies." McCormick did not pursue the issue, which would be left for Marcus to deal with during cross-examination.

Kent testified that if children with a language handicap were placed in the same class as those who already spoke English, both groups would suffer. The teacher would have the choice of focusing on those with poorer language skills, to the detriment of the English-speaking children, or focusing on the more proficient children, which would harm the others. Therefore, the Spanish-speaking children actually benefited from segregation and the undivided attention of their English-speaking teachers. If both groups of children were in the same school, they would have to be separated anyway, for pedagogical reasons. Most parents understood that, Kent stated, and he repeated Holden's claim that no one but Mrs. Ochoa had ever expressed dissatisfaction with the system.

Ogle must have realized that this line of questioning was not helpful, because he jumped in and took over from Holden. He elicited the fact that, in Kent's words, Hoover had the same facilities as the other schools in the district, "with the additional facilities of showers, and we furnish them with towels, soap. . . . We have felt that the children of the Mexican homes do not have the facilities in their homes, so we have made it available to them. They are not forced to take their showers, but we recommend it, and we have tried to carry on a program of health hygiene, and have made these facilities available for the children, and they are using them." Under Ogle's guidance, Kent repeatedly emphasized that separate schools were a pedagogical necessity.

Then it was Marcus's turn to cross-examine, and he was able to show that Kent believed that the real problem was being Mexican-American.

> Q: Mr. Kent, in your opinion, is a child retarded because of the fact that he speaks or is a bilingual, in other words, speaks Spanish and English?
>
> A: That is one of the factors, yes, sir.
>
> Q: Now, isn't it a fact, Mr. Kent, that a child has a more comprehensive knowledge, at least linguistically speaking, because of the fact that he is able to speak both Spanish and English?
>
> A: I would say not.
>
> Q: You would say not. Do you say a person who speaks three or four or five different languages was not as advanced as a person who spoke only one language?
>
> A: Well, it depends on what you are trying to do . . . we are trying to arrive at an educational cultivation of our American ideals. . . . And when they come with a bilingual or a trilingual handicap, it makes it much harder for them, in comparison with the other children.
>
> Q: You mean to say because the child speaks the English and the Spanish language the child cannot understand the American ideals?
>
> A: . . . It doesn't mean that he cannot, but it does mean in the teaching of these ideals it makes a great handicap for him, because he has to start with that handicap of forgetting what he has learned the first six years of his life or seven years, or wherever he starts, and he has to start out on our culture.

Kent hedged when questioned about whether he considered Mexicans to be less intelligent than others, but Marcus persisted, and Kent finally stated that the Mexican child, on average, "is lower intellectually than the child of Anglo-Saxon descent." He based the statement on the results of IQ tests, but he explained away any results that showed Mexican-American students with high IQs. A child with an IQ of 120, which Kent described as "genius class," "could still have a mental age of three years old." That was because an IQ test "shows a potentiality of holding knowledge" but "doesn't mean they have acquired that knowledge." Judge McCormick asked whether it might not be wise to put a Mexican-American student with a high IQ into a school with others who had comparable IQs. Kent was reluctant to respond, but McCormick, too, persisted, and Kent finally stated that there "would naturally be a feeling of inferiority, to put him with children of a higher economic standpoint and to be in competition with children who have had this training in the American way of living. . . . That child may have that mental age and mental I.Q., but may not have that ability to work, nor that desire to work." Assuming there would be only one such Mexican-American student in an integrated class, Kent added, "It is very hard for one child to compete with 40 children of another race in a class."

Judge McCormick asked what factors other than "the social attitudes and the industrial inclination" were relevant.

"There would be moral factors, hygienic," Kent replied. "There would be the economic status of the child to be considered, his social place in the community."

What was meant by "economic and social status in the community?" McCormick queried.

Kent replied that children from "a low economic home" could not participate as fully as others in "functions which they go on during the class year." He continued:

> For instance, I have a cooking class where there are 24 white or Anglo-Saxon children and there are two Mexican children, and they can't bring the equipment, their hands are not clean when they come, and the teacher always has to ask them, "Did you wash your hands?" She tries to do it diplomatically, but the other children see them. Then they don't have the facilities they need to work with. For instance, if they are going to make biscuits, they can't bring the equipment, their parents won't let them have it, and it is an embarrassing thing for them.

Why all the children in a cooking class were not asked to wash their hands was not discussed. Kent reiterated his point about embarrassment:

> In one school which I had, we had Mexican children in it, and I noticed when I went there that they ate at one end of the play-

ground, and the other children ate at the other end. I moved the two tables together, and they didn't like it at all, because the Mexican children didn't want the Anglo-Saxon children to know that they ate tortillas, and I had eventually to move the children apart, to do away with their embarrassment, and I have had them feel inferior because of the clothing they wear, too, sir.

Ogle jumped in again to ask whether Kent's fear was what "the children might do by reason of their undiplomatic handling of any situation that might arise" if a child were taken out of "a Mexican group" and placed with others.

"Yes, it is that," Kent said, at which point Judge McCormick asked whether it wouldn't be the duty of the school authorities "to endeavor to inculcate into the disrespectful Anglo-Saxon child some respect for the other child?" "I don't think it would be disrespect," Kent responded. "I think it would be just a natural thing that develops."

Kent was dismissed, and Holden called Edith M. Gilbert to the stand. She had been the principal of the Fremont School in Santa Ana for twenty-two years and told the court that the school was a happy place. There had been no complaints about children being assigned there except those from the two witnesses. "The rest of them, they are very happy," she said, adding that the Fremont School was always first in attendance in the Santa Ana district. Cross-examined by Marcus, Mrs. Gilbert said that Fremont reading classes were "in most cases above the average norm" on standardized tests "in nearly every grade, and in every class this year." Nonetheless, she maintained that the students' bewildering insistence on speaking Spanish disadvantaged them. "[The child] may come to you in the kindergarten, but he speaks Spanish all the time at home, and his playmates speak Spanish to him all the time. When I go down the street, I hear Spanish spoken far more than I do English, and then we say to them, 'Why don't you speak English?' But they don't, and that is a language handicap which is very hard to overcome."

Marcus, perhaps stupefied at the contradictions implicit in Gilbert's testimony, ended his questioning of her. Holden next called Robert H. Reinhard, Santa Ana's assistant superintendent of schools. He not only denied telling Mrs. Fuentes that Mexican children were dirty but also claimed, "I have never had any conversation with Mrs.

Fuentes." Still, it would be unfortunate to put the children into the Franklin School, because "the three Mexican schools are the only schools that offer shower facilities to the children." The shower at Franklin had been converted into a nurse's closet. In addition, Franklin already had about thirty-four pupils per teacher, which was higher than the city average. If it took more students, it would have to give up its library-auditorium or teachers' workroom. Again, there was no suggestion that the school numbers could be equalized by placing all the children in specific grades in one of the schools. Richard F. Harris, the Westminster superintendent, was recalled to state that he had never told Méndez that Mexicans were dirty. With that, court was adjourned until the next morning.

CHAPTER 7

The Experts Testify

July 11, 1945, was the last day of the trial. Holden recalled Frank A. Henderson, superintendent of the Santa Ana school district, to make the arguments that Mexican-American students were sent to the school closest to them, that Fremont (the "Mexican" school) was a good institution, and that segregation served Mexican-American students well.

Henderson went over a map of Santa Ana to demonstrate that the composition of the schools reflected the ethnicity of the people living in each district. Fremont, for example, was in an area where about 95 percent of the population was Mexican. Yes, he said, non-Mexican-American children were allowed to transfer out of the district: "We transfer some children to some of these schools if they are in an extremely small minority in the school of their district, in order for the good of the child, as we see it." The students' ancestry was determined by "simple observation" for African-Americans and on the basis of their names for others. The district had transferred two or three "colored children" from Fremont, where they were the only African-American students, to Franklin, "where almost 100 percent of the colored children are found." Fremont was nevertheless a fine school. Reflecting the unstated expectation that Mexican-Americans would work only at menial trades, he emphasized that Fremont had "a very nice little cottage, which is used for cooking and sewing training, and home-making in that school." In addition, "We have a rather good manual training shop for boys in the Fremont School," but there were no such facilities at Franklin. The Delhi School also had a bungalow used to teach shop: "That is a Mexican School, so-called." At most, the non-Mexican schools had "a little set of tools" on "a little rack." Clearly, Mexican-American students were being prepared for low-paying manual work; just as clearly, other children were not.

Pressed by Judge McCormick, Henderson asserted that decisions about who could transfer to another school, and particularly decisions that allowed non-Spanish-speaking children in the Fremont district to transfer to Franklin, were made on an ad hoc basis rather than in accordance with any board policy. He agreed that every non-Spanish-speaking child who asked to be transferred was given permission to do so. The reason, he asserted, as Marcus picked up the questioning, was that Fremont would be bad for such children because they would not be able to communicate with their Spanish-speaking playmates.

Marcus completed his cross-examination, Holden elicited once again Henderson's statement that he would be willing to transfer any student who had "a good reason," and the defense rested. The court recessed for lunch, and when it reconvened, the plaintiffs presented their rebuttal witnesses. Ogle was apparently coaching Holden a bit too loudly by that time, for at one point Marcus interrupted his questioning to ask if Ogle had something he wanted to say.

The first rebuttal witness was eighteen-year-old Isabel Ayala, from Garden Grove. Her home was five blocks from Lincoln and about a mile and a half to two miles from Hoover, which meant that her two younger sisters had to walk two and a half blocks and then get on the Hoover school bus. When the family moved to Garden Grove in 1943, Isabel took her sisters to enroll in Lincoln. She spoke first with the Lincoln principal and then, almost a year later, with Superintendent Kent, who told her that all students of Mexican ancestry had to go to Hoover because of language problems. She protested that her sisters, born in the United States, spoke very good English. Kent's rejoinder was that if he let them in, most of the other Mexican children would want to come too. He did not speak with her sisters or give them any examination. The seven-year-old girl was put in the second grade, and she performed so well that her teacher wanted to skip her to the third grade. Replying to a question from Judge McCormick, Ayala testified that her parents spoke Spanish and some English but that the children "don't even speak in Spanish around the house." Ayala, who was obviously fluent in English, told the court that she had left high school after three years and, at the time of the trial, was working in a local department store — the kind of path followed by many other young Mexican-Americans.

The two most important rebuttal witnesses called by Marcus were

Ralph L. Beals and Marie H. Hughes. Professor Beals was chair of the Department of Anthropology at the University of California–Los Angeles. He had done research in Mexico for the National Research Council and the Smithsonian Institution as well as for the university, and he had written roughly thirty books and articles. What he had found, he said, was that neither learning English nor becoming Americanized was best accomplished by segregation; in fact, the best way to learn a language was through immersion with people who spoke it.

Marcus asked whether segregating the Mexican-American students served a valid purpose. The answer, Dr. Beals replied, depended on whether the objective was "to provide a better education for the Mexican groups" or "preparing these Mexican students to become assimilated into the general curricular milieu of the United States" – that is, Americanization. "Certainly, in the latter case," he continued,

> it would seem to me that the objectives would not be best obtained by segregation. As a matter of fact, the learning of adequate English, it seems to me, would be interfered with by a program of segregation . . . keeping Mexican and Spanish-speaking children together simply means they talk Spanish together and do not learn English as rapidly as if they were associating with English-speaking people. . . . Segregation defeats the purpose of teaching English, certainly, to the Spanish-speaking child . . . if these children were children of Spanish-speaking families, and you gave them all their training in a segregated group, they would continue to converse in Spanish.

Although that conclusion might seem obvious from the vantage point of the twenty-first century, it was far less so to the Orange County educators of the mid-twentieth century. In any event, Marcus's purpose was not to convince them but to show Judge McCormick that segregation was not, as the districts alleged, beneficial for the Mexican-American children.

Segregation also impeded "the assimilation of the child to American customs and ways," Beals said. "In terms of making the children familiar with the whole body of customs, and so much of which is unexpressed, in our way of behavior or learning such as the attitudes of the Anglo-speaking peoples . . . towards various subjects or knowing what the attitudes of even children of their own age are towards various subjects, there can be no substitute, in my opinion, for actual contact with Anglo-speaking people, and rather intimate contact."

Judge McCormick interjected, saying, "What I conceive to be the fundamental principle of public school education in the United States, [is] the general commingling of children of all ancestries and descents for the purpose of building up a culture of our own. That is what I conceive to be the Americanization aspect of public school instruction." That is precisely what Beals testified would not be achieved by segregation.

Marcus returned to the matter of English proficiency. Was it best for both English-speaking and Spanish-speaking children to be segregated?

A: In my opinion, it is not to the advantage of the pupils, and regardless of linguistic background. . . . This is precisely the period [between grades one and six or one and eight] when the [Spanish-speaking] child would get its best control in English, if it had the fullest possible exposure to it, and segregation defeats the purpose of teaching English, certainly, to the Spanish-speaking child.

Q: Now, with respect to children who do speak the English language, of Mexican descent, would it be to their best interests to educate them separately from other children by compelling them to attend schools solely attended by children of Mexican descent?

A: In that case I think it would be to their definite disadvantage. . . . If they have a command of English to start with, they probably would, in terms of a number of studies that have been made, and the chances are very strong that if they were put in with groups that were somewhat deficient in their English speech, that they would actually lose some of their English facility during that time.

What effect would such segregation have "with respect to their cultural development or their Americanization?" Marcus asked. Beals's answer forecast the testimony that would be given by Dr. Kenneth

Clark in *Brown v. Board of Education* about the negative psychological effects of segregation:

Well, I think it would be very unfortunate for them. Judging by some studies that have been made under my direction . . . a feeling of antagonism is built up in children, when they are segregated in this fashion. They actually become hostile to the whole culture of the surrounding majority group, as a result of the segregation, which appears to be, to them at least, discrimination. . . . The disadvantage of segregation, it would seem to me, would come primarily from the reinforcing of stereotypes of inferiority-superiority, which exists in the population as a whole. The advantages [of desegregation], properly handled, would come, then, in the breaking down of those stereotypes and in the broadening of understanding of people of different cultural background and the understanding of different cultures.

Ogle cross-examined Beals only briefly, apparently deciding—quite correctly, as it turned out—that nothing beneficial to the defendants would come out of his testimony. Judge McCormick had been listening closely, and he asked what would happen if children with varying degrees of facility in English were mixed together. Wouldn't that be better, in terms of Americanization, than segregation? Yes, Beals replied, "with regard to the Americanization program, the mixed group would become much more rapidly aware of the main trends in American life."

Marcus had not met the plaintiffs' final witness, who had been brought in by National Lawyers Guild attorney Charles Christopher. It was therefore Christopher who questioned Marie Hughes. Hughes, called as an expert witness, was a Ph.D. candidate at Stanford University. She had been a school principal and curriculum director in New Mexico for nineteen years and had worked in Los Angeles County for the past five. Hughes was a specialist on inter-American education for the American Council on Education's Intergroup Education Project. More to the point, she had specialized in research about Mexican-American children for twenty years, and Christopher began by asking her whether segregation served Orange County students well. "It is not to the best interests of children in America, Orange County or not, to work and play together and go to school together under segregated conditions," Hughes said firmly. She agreed with Beals that Spanish-speaking children learn English better in an integrated setting.

Q: What is the effect of placing children of Mexican descent in one school separate and apart from children not of Mexican descent, as to their achievement and ability to learn the English language?

A: Children learn a language through hearing it and through having a motive, a reason, for using it. Therefore, children who speak another language, such as Spanish, when in association with children speaking English have a reason to learn and to speak English. Moreover, they hear English spoken, and you cannot learn a language and learn to speak it well without hearing it. They hear it on the playground and in informal situations, multiple situations, in both contact with their own peers, that is, their own age-mates. . . . There is no doubt, in my judgment, that children in the mixed schools, that is, children in association with Anglo-American children learn English much faster and much more expertly than they do in a segregated school. . . . The best way always to teach English is to give many opportunities to speak English, to hear it spoken correctly, and have reasons for speaking it, and to enlarge the experiences which demand English . . . if your experiences are limited, your vocabulary will be limited.

Guided by Christopher, she too talked about the psychological results of segregation, as well as its effect on Americanization. She referred to the research she had done for her master's thesis, studying first-grade students in both segregated and nonsegregated schools.

A: Segregation, by its very nature, is a reminder constantly of inferiority, of not being wanted, of not being a part of the community. Such an experience cannot possibly build the best personality or the sort of person who is most at home in the world, and able to contribute and live well. . . . I would say that any separation of children which prevents free communication among them, on an equal basis, that is, a peer basis, would be bad because of the very fact that segregation tends to give an aura of inferiority. In order to have the people of the United States understand one another, it is necessary for them to live together, as it were, and the public school is the one mechanism where all the children of all the people go.

Q: Aside from the language handicap and their rate of learning it, what other effects on the children are there resulting from segregation of the Mexican pupils, as opposed to the mixed schools?

A: I think the result of segregating Mexican pupils is that by putting [them] in a group of people with their own kind only, . . . they tend to learn only the ways of that group and to feel not at home with others, not to have confidence, and not to have the know-all, that is, they do not know the conventions and the ways of living of the larger group.

Segregation, Hughes stated, cemented insularism.

Ogle declined to cross-examine. Judge McCormick asked about experiments to back up Hughes's assertions, and she referred again to her own experience:

I worked in a segregated school last year for five weeks with a group of youngsters . . . to determine their measure of English . . . and that report is to be released this fall. . . . The lack of English ability is just indescribable in children living under such conditions [segregated schools]. The holes in their language is something that is appalling. Even when it comes to the meaning of common vegetables, fifth grade children don't know even all of that, because they haven't had an opportunity in informal contacts to learn that.

"They were all normal children, were they?" McCormick asked, referring to the children in the segregated schools. "I mean they were not children who were arrested mentally?"

"No," Hughes replied. And with that, both the plaintiffs and the defendants ended their questioning.

Judge McCormick told the two sides that he wanted briefs from both of them. He was particularly interested in having them first discuss the question of jurisdiction: was this a case appropriately before a federal court? He was not at all certain that it was: "It is my view, without any decision in the matter, that education is not a Federal matter, that education is a State matter, and if it is, that may determine the case." Second, he wanted their thoughts about whether segregation was necessarily the equivalent of discrimination. He also expected them to make the arguments for and against the case being treated as a class action and then indicate what, if any, relief should be granted to the plaintiffs. He was clearly not looking for a mass of paper. "The briefs should be brief," he admonished. Finally, he asked the two attorneys to submit draft language for the findings of fact and conclusions of law — what the trial had shown the facts to be and what decision the relevant laws dictated, in light of those facts. He would use that language as a starting point for whatever his decision might be.

The brief Marcus presented to the court on September 28, 1945, eleven weeks after the trial ended, was organized so that it answered each of Judge McCormick's questions in turn. There was no doubt the court had jurisdiction, Marcus wrote, as federal law specifically empowered federal courts to hear cases involving deprivation of a person's privileges and immunities, or a person's equal rights, by a state. The plaintiffs were not claiming that there was a federal right to attend public schools, because the provision of public schools was a matter for the state. Once the state established a system of public schools, however, the people of the state had a federally protected right to the "equal protection of the laws" — that is, to be treated equally in their access to the schools. Orange County admitted that it was segregating Mexican-American children, Marcus continued, and it now had the burden of proving that the segregation was justified. In his view, the segregation had an "unreasonable, unjust, and discriminatory basis." As Marcus sought to show that the segregation was discriminatory, his anger at Superintendent Kent's testimony became clear. "Mr. Kent told the Court that Mexicans are inferior to the 'white' in matters of personal hygiene, in their ability, in their economic outlook, their clothing and ability to take part in school activities," he wrote. "This witness throughout his testimony has demonstrated an attitude of racial superiority such as that of Hitler combined with and productive of the belief that, at least as to Mexican inferiors, the State, acting through School Boards and School Superintendents, has the right and duty to determine whether the child should be allowed to exercise its constitutional rights to be treated as other children are and to enjoy the same privileges." Referring to the "Franklin School, where the alleged super-race pupils are ensconced and safeguarded," he argued that "the mental attitude and bureaucratic psychology of Mr. Kent also pervade the Boards of Education, and this is the real reason for the complete segregation of the American-Mexican children." Marcus juxtaposed Kent's ideas, and those of the school board, with American ideals:

> Mr. Kent's and the respondents' ism, whatever it may be called, is at war with the American idea of equality and the democratic ideals declared in the bill of rights. . . . Juan Munoz told Mr. Emley, Superintendent of the Garden Grove Schools, "I am fighting for my children's rights." . . . American-Mexicans are unable to understand why their children should be segregated. For example, Mrs. Fuentes, in her endeavor to have her boy received in the Franklin School in Santa Ana, asked why her children, of Mexican descent, are not given "the same rights" and taught "just the same" and allowed to "mingle with the Americans right along with the citizens of the United States, as I am."
>
> This plain question speaks a volume. It depicts the injured and embarrassed feeling of Mexican parents, which must be reflected and magnified in the children who are the direct victims of the discrimination; it portrays a yearning for being taken into American life and fellowship and the despair which comes from realization of the sad reality that they are now a people apart from, and subject to a purported race who assume superiority.

Turning to Superintendent Harris, Marcus waxed sarcastic. "According to this erudite educator," the Mexican child does not know the Mother Goose rhymes and "must have 'a specially trained teacher' . . . [because he was not] endowed with an education and Mother Goose cultural background. It would be interesting to take a poll of the judiciary or use a questionnaire to discover how much or how little they are thus endowed." If lack of a thorough grounding in Mother Goose were the criterion, he asked, "what of the children of Portuguese descent, or German or French or Italian or Greek lineage . . . and Filipinos and Japanese," none of whom were sent to Hoover?

The discriminatory segregation also violated "the rights and duties of parents" by ignoring the parents' requests to have their children transferred. Marcus cited statutes and cases demonstrating that California law recognized "the parent's authority and responsibility for the child's welfare." The Orange County school boards were making it impossible for the parents to carry out that responsibility. Finally, California and federal law authorized class-action suits when, as here, "the question is one of a common or general interest, of many persons," and it authorized the granting of injunctions preventing the continuation of the behavior. Marcus's conclusion invoked not only President Franklin D. Roosevelt's State of the Union address of January 1941, in which he spoke of "four essential human freedoms" (freedom of speech and religion and freedom from want and fear) and World War II, but international relations as well. He did so with the kind of rhetorical flourishes seldom encountered in legal briefs:

> Of what avail is our theory of democracy if the principles of equal rights, of equal protection and equal obligations are not practiced? . . . Of what use are the four freedoms if freedom is not allowed? Of what avail are the thousands upon thousands of lives of Mexican-Americans who sacrificed their all for their country in this great "War of Freedom" if freedom of education is denied them? Of what avail is our "education" if the system that propounds it denies the equality of all? . . . The indelible imprint of mass discrimination of pseudo theories of intellectual superiority upon the minds and lives of innocent children decries the principles of democracy, freedom and justice. . . . The decision of this Court is of tremendous importance. The burden cast upon this Court involves the lives, future happiness of uncounted thousands of American citizens. Eager eyes and attentive ears North and South of our borders await the result. We cannot fail them.

On October 1 the two amici, the Los Angeles chapter of the National Lawyers Guild and the ACLU's Southern California branch, filed a brief written by Christopher and Wirin. Because McCormick had indicated doubts about federal jurisdiction in a case involving education, much of the brief was devoted to cases holding that federal courts did have jurisdiction in cases alleging violations of Fourteenth

Amendment rights. The brief relied heavily on the Supreme Court's recent decision in *West Virginia State Board of Education v. Barnette* (1943), quoting the Court's statement that "the Fourteenth Amendment . . . protects the citizens against the state itself and all of its creatures — Boards of Education not excepted." The brief argued as well that the admitted segregation was "arbitrary, discriminatory and unjust," and quoted the Supreme Court's holding in *Korematsu v. United States* that "all legal restrictions which curtail the civil rights of a single racial group are immediately suspect."

The matter of jurisdiction was crucial to Orange County, and much of the brief the defendants filed on October 17 was devoted to that subject. The court lacked jurisdiction because education is a matter for the states alone, Holden wrote, and a state had fulfilled its obligation to its citizens when it provided an education in equal facilities. The brief cited cases such as *Gong Lum v. Rice,* in which the Supreme Court had ruled that a Chinese-American student could be denied admission to a Mississippi "white" school and sent instead to a school for African-Americans. The cases he relied on, Holden acknowledged, were cases involving race and were therefore different from *Mendez.* Nonetheless, the Supreme Court had held that separate but equal accommodations were constitutional. Moreover, there was no state action here. "School districts are mere administrative agencies of the state," and what they did could not be considered actions by the state. Admittedly, Superintendent Kent had erred in not finding out whether the Ochoa and Sianez children spoke English, but that was a mistake of an employee rather than state action.

The real question, Holden asked rhetorically and in capital letters, was "WHERE A SCHOOL DISTRICT HAS CLASSIFIED PUPILS INTO TWO CLASSES AND HAS FURNISHED TO EACH CLASS EXACTLY THE SAME EDUCATION AT EQUALLY CONVENIENT LOCATIONS, HAS SUCH DISTRICT VIOLATED ANY PROVISION OF THE UNITED STATES CONSTITUTION OR ANY LAW OF THE UNITED STATES?" His answer: "If it be the law, which has been held to be in all cases before the courts, that a colored citizen has not been denied the equal protection of the laws where he has been given an equal education with others although at a different location, how can it be held that a citizen of any other race would be denied equal protection of the laws under the same circumstances?"

The segregation did not result in discrimination, Holden claimed. If Mexican-Americans wanted to go to other schools, they could move. Referencing the Fremont School in Santa Ana, Holden noted that most of the people living in the Fremont zone were Mexican-Americans. His approach to the placing of schools in the heart of Mexican-American neighborhoods, which ensured segregation, was an interesting one. "How can it be considered unjust or arbitrary," he asked, "for the Board to locate one of the finest school plants in the District right in the community inhabited by people of Mexican descent? Was it unjust to provide that community with a civic center and playgrounds for civic activities and recreation?" In any event, segregation was the students' fault, or that of their parents: most of the Spanish-speaking students in Garden Grove's Hoover school district "are segregated by their own act of living in the community surrounding the Hoover School, and only 13 of them are segregated by reason of the rule of the School Board."

The plaintiffs, defendants, and amici submitted reply briefs that essentially repeated their earlier arguments. Then the community sat back to wait and see what Judge McCormick would say. The wait was a lengthy one.

CHAPTER 8

Judge McCormick Decides

Judge McCormick handed down his opinion, labeled "Conclusions of the Court," on February 18, 1946, seven months after the trial ended. The length of time between trial and decision suggests that McCormick, well aware of the landmark nature of what he was about to do, had given it a great deal of thought.

From the plaintiffs' point of view, the wait was worth it. The verdict was a resounding victory — one that upheld all the plaintiffs' arguments and, to a large extent, tracked David Marcus's brief in the case.

Judge McCormick first addressed the jurisdiction issue and the claim that because education was purely a state matter, the case should not be decided by a federal court. Education was indeed a state matter, he said, but not exclusively so. He quoted the 1899 U.S. Supreme Court case of *Cumming v. Board of Education*, in which the Court held that "*any interference on the part of Federal authority with the management of such schools cannot be justified except in the case of a clear and unmistakable disregard of rights secured by the supreme law of the land.*" (The italics were added by Judge McCormick.) California had control over funding for the public schools, teachers' qualifications, the admission of pupils, the curriculum, and school boards and superintendents, so there was no question that education was a state matter. In other words, if the state, or an official under its control, was exercising its power over education in such a way as to violate rights protected by the Fourteenth Amendment's equal protection clause, the federal courts could intervene. McCormick repeated the phrase from *West Virginia v. Barnette* that had been quoted in Marcus's brief: "The Fourteenth Amendment, as now applied to the States, protects the citizen against the State itself and all of its creatures — Boards of Education not excepted." The question therefore became whether the segregation in Orange County violated the equal protection clause. First, however, McCormick would consider whether the segregation violated California's own laws. He held that it did.

California law required school districts to admit all children over age six, whether or not their parents were American citizens, and to maintain elementary schools "with equal rights and privileges as far as possible." That, Judge McCormick declared, applied to all children "regardless of their ancestry or extraction" (with the notable exception of Indian and Asian children), and it meant that segregation of "pupils of Mexican ancestry" was prohibited. "The common segregation and practices of the school authorities in the defendant school districts in Orange County," however, "pertain solely to children of Mexican ancestry and parentage. They are singled out as a class for segregation." Such segregation violated the state's own laws.

California wanted students to be integrated, according to Judge McCormick's reading of its laws. He found it "noteworthy that the educational advantages of their commingling with other pupils [are] regarded as being so important to the school system of the State" that education was mandatory for both citizens and noncitizens. California law reflected "a clear purpose to avoid and forbid distinctions among pupils based upon race or ancestry." Further, the Supreme Court had declared in *Hirabayashi* that such distinctions were " 'by their very nature odious to a free people whose institutions are founded upon the doctrine of equality' " and " 'utterly inconsistent with American traditions and ideals.' "

Interestingly, it was only when quoting *Hirabayashi* that McCormick turned to federal constitutional law. What makes that interesting is the fact that McCormick could have ruled simply that state law did not permit the segregation of Mexican-Americans, and ended the discussion there. Judges usually prefer to decide cases on the basis of a statute rather than get into constitutional issues. If Judge McCormick thought the constitutional issue was a key one, however, he could have turned to it immediately and omitted any discussion of the state law. As McCormick was about to hold that the segregation of Mexican-American students violated federal law, there was no need for him to get involved in state statutes. Why, then, did he do so?

There are two possibilities. McCormick might have begun the trial with questions about the illegitimacy of the segregation, but as the later passages in his opinion indicated, he was now convinced that segregation was both unconstitutional and counterproductive. In addition, he clearly doubted that the school board's motives had anything to do with good pedagogy. It is therefore possible that he wanted to chastise the boards as violators not only of federal law but also of the very state laws from which they derived their authority.

A second possibility is that the contentiousness of the issue and the groundbreaking nature of his decision led McCormick to assume, correctly, that the case would be appealed. No judge likes to have his or her rulings overturned by a higher court. Might McCormick have been concerned that the Ninth Circuit Court of Appeals would be more unwilling than he to confront the "separate but equal" doctrine, and so he wanted to give it a less radical ground on which to decide? If so, he was prescient.

In any event, Judge McCormick concluded his discussion of "the utter irreconcilability of the segregation practices" with California law and went on to suggest a new interpretation of the federal equal protection clause. " 'The equal protection of the laws' pertaining to the public school system in California," he wrote, "is not provided by furnishing in separate schools the same technical facilities, text books and courses of instruction to children of Mexican ancestry that are available to the other public school children regardless of their ancestry." It was, of course, not the case that Mexican-American children were given the same facilities, books, or curriculum, but for the purposes of making the argument that segregation was unconstitutional, that Marcus had agreed to ignore those differences. Then came McCormick's formulation, which was so radical for its day: "A paramount requisite in the American system of public education is social equality. It must be open to all children by unified school association regardless of lineage." That, simply stated, was a declaration that "separate but equal" was not equal. The language must have made the parties to the litigation catch their breath at its boldness. McCormick was implicitly denying the legitimacy of an entire body of equal protection law as it applied to education, and he was doing so in language that would soon have civil rights organizations all over the country rushing into the case.

The only permissible grounds for the Orange County segregation, McCormick continued, were the children's language difficulties. "But even such situations do not justify the general and continuous segregation in separate schools of the children of Mexican ancestry from the rest of the elementary school population as has been shown to be the practice in the defendant school districts." Instead, there must be a "credible examination" of each child, "regardless of his ethnic traits or ancestry." No such examination existed here. In Santa Ana, for example, any tests given to entering children were "generally hasty, superficial and not reliable. In some instances," McCormick continued with indignation, placement was based on "the Latinized or Mexican name of the child," even though "such methods of evaluating language knowledge are illusory and are not conducive to the inculcation and enjoyment of civil rights which are of primary importance in the public school system of education in the United States." That sentence effectively asserted that civil rights and knowledge about them were key goals of American public education, and so was avoidance of artificial distinctions among the students. McCormick had clearly been attentive to the testimony of Ralph Beals and Marie Hughes, the plaintiffs' two expert witnesses.

> The evidence clearly shows that Spanish-speaking children are retarded in learning English by lack of exposure to its use because of segregation, and that commingling of the entire student body instills and develops a common cultural attitude among the school children which is imperative for the perpetuation of American institutions and ideals. It is also established by the record that the methods of segregation prevalent in the defendant school districts foster antagonisms in the children and suggest inferiority among them where none exists.

As a "flagrant" example of "the discriminatory results of segregation," McCormick cited the Lincoln and Roosevelt schools in El Modena. He drew on Superintendent Hammarsten's testimony that a recent seventh-grade class at segregated Lincoln was a superior one, but even the outstanding students in the class had not been moved to Roosevelt. Although there was no evidence that class members had asked to be transferred, McCormick noted, "the record does show without contradiction that another class" — Carol Torres's class — had protested against the segregation to no avail.

Judge McCormick discussed each of the districts in turn, making it clear that he held them all equally accountable. Their actions, he concluded, reflected "a clear purpose to arbitrarily discriminate against the pupils of Mexican ancestry and to deny to them the equal protection of the laws."

What Judge McCormick did was sufficiently revolutionary to deserve emphasis here. He not only restated the Supreme Court's suggestion in *Hirabayashi* that discrimination based on ancestry was usually suspect; he also applied that doctrine in declaring a state's actions to be illegal. He held that Mexican-Americans as a group were protected by the Fourteenth Amendment and could not legitimately be discriminated against — a holding that would not be echoed by the U.S. Supreme Court until 1954. He declared that school segregation impeded learning instead of enhancing it. He insisted, as the NAACP would argue in *Brown v. Board of Education*, that segregated schools fostered unwarranted feelings of inferiority in the students who were segregated. Most important, of course, he declared that "separate but equal" education was a violation of the Fourteenth Amendment. There again, he anticipated the Supreme Court by almost a decade.

As noted earlier, Judge McCormick had asked both sides in the case to submit draft language on findings of fact and conclusions of law that would enable him to flesh out his opinion, making clear his step-by-step reasoning. A detailed catalog of his thinking would make his decision more likely to be upheld by a higher court. Marcus and Holden had done as Judge McCormick requested, and on March 21 he elaborated on his decision in documents entitled "Findings of Fact and Conclusions of Law" and "Judgment and Injunction." "It is true," he began paragraph after paragraph, reiterating, for example, that all children of Mexican descent had been segregated and that, as American citizens, they were entitled to attend public schools "without segregation or discrimination." He repeated the points made in his decision and added, "It is true" that the four school districts had acted with a "common plan, design and purpose" — that is, they had conspired to discriminate against the children. The school districts were permanently enjoined from continuing the segregation and ordered to pay court costs of $56 each. On March 26 the school districts filed objections to Judge McCormick's "Findings of Fact and Conclusions of Law." McCormick had not mentioned that, in the districts' words, "the facilities provided in each of the schools are identical." He had, in effect, conceded as much in his initial opinion, and the districts argued that if the facilities were identical, there was no violation of the equal protection clause and federal courts lacked jurisdiction. Apparently, Holden was eager to have the acknowledgment of equal facilities emphasized in the record that would go to the appeals court because, by then, the districts had definitely decided to appeal. McCormick overruled the objections three days later. The case was ready to move to the Ninth Circuit Court of Appeals, sitting in San Francisco.

Suddenly, *Mendez* was news. "L.A. Federal Judge Issues Injunction Against Local Schools," the *Orange Daily News* trumpeted in a large front-page headline. "Ruling Gives Mexican Children Equal Rights," the *Los Angeles Times* echoed. The *Santa Ana Register* soon reported, "County Schools to Appeal U.S. Segregation Ruling," quoting Ogle as saying that if necessary, he was prepared to appeal the case all the way to the U.S. Supreme Court. The county, and some of the school districts, would not give up without a fight.

There was a difference in the way the various districts handled the matter before the case reached the appeals court, however. Westminster integrated its two elementary schools at the beginning of the 1946–1947 academic year, putting grades one through four in Westminster Main and grades five through eight in Hoover. Finally, the Méndez children were enrolled in Westminster Main. El Modena chose to play hardball, in spite of Judge McCormick's injunction against continuing the segregation. The minutes of its September 13 school board meeting made it clear that the district would not change its policies and would continue to give Mexican-American school-children a later starting time so that they could work the walnut harvest. According to the *Orange Daily News*, Holden had informed the boards, incorrectly, that they were required to do nothing until the appeals court acted. Mexican-American parents in El Modena, however, had created the Unity League of El Modena (it soon became the Latin American League of El Modena), and they were ready to demand their rights. A number of them went to another school board meeting on September 17, at which the board agreed to test all children ready to enter the first grade. Presumably, those who spoke English would not be segregated. That did nothing for the children already in the school, and the board's language indicated that it was unwilling to do more.

It would soon have to change that position, however. Alexander Lievanos, who owned a small shop in El Modena, had tried and failed to enroll his son at Roosevelt. On September 27, with the help of the Latin American Organization (LAO), Lievanos filed a petition asking Judge McCormick to hold Hammarsten and the school board in contempt. The judge issued an order the same day, requiring the defendants to appear before him by October 14. Other parents were turning to the courts as well. On September 28 Judge Leon Yankwich issued a different contempt citation against the El Modena board for transferring a Mexican-American student from Roosevelt to Lincoln. That was the situation when the board met again on October 9. By then, Lievanos had been elected chairman of the newly organized Unity League of El Modena, and the league asked him to appear before the board to see whether a joint plan to end the segregation could be devised. Other parents also attended, as did organizer Fred W. Ross and *Latin American* editor Hector Tarango, who had helped find plaintiffs for *Mendez*. The secretary recorded the ensuing discussion as follows:

MR. SEIJAS: I believe we tried to discuss that [a plan for desegregation] at the last meeting but Mr. Hammarsten just laughed at us. . . .

MR. NEIGER [a member of the board]: . . . We did discuss a plan of changing schools, but we have the question of a budget. . . .

MR. ROSS: You understand why Latin American parents want their children to mingle with the Anglo Saxon children?

MR. NEIGER: But there are many more Latin American children going here than white children.

MR. ROSS: Well, what I meant was that English was a second language to them and if they associated with English speaking children more they would learn to speak much better.

MR. NEIGER: If the parents had English as the language spoken in the home the children would have no trouble when they got to school and would do much better. . . .

MR. DURANGO [This appears to be a misspelling of Hector Tarango's name.]: When you give the tests do you give them to the Anglo children too? What would you do if one of them failed the test?

MR. HAMMARSTEN: We have never had that problem. . . . The children themselves don't want to be put in with the others. It is only the parents who don't know what is best for them. We had a girl last year come to Roosevelt from Lincoln, she stayed only a few day[s] and was very unhappy away from her friends, and the work was ahead of her and she couldn't keep up. She was very happy to go back over to Lincoln.

MR. VEGA: You waited too long to let her come into the other school, if she had been there from the start she would have been all right.

MR. CAMPBELL [another board member]: There is only a very small percentage that want to change schools.

MR. VEGA: I beg your pardon. We have a petition with 98 per cent of the signatures of the people in El Modena.

MR. CAMPBELL: . . . Some of the Mexican American parents have said they do not want their children to go to school with the other Mexican children. You still have to separate them some way and our teachers have found this way is best and we have been doing it for 25 years.

MR. DURANGO: . . . You cannot compare now with 25 years ago when our parents who came from Mexico were here. You are dealing with second and third generation[s] of Mexican Americans now. So you cannot use 25 year old records to compare our children with. You haven't tried to combine the classes in the present time.

Superintendent Hammarsten objected that no thought was being given to the parents who did not want their children to attend school with other Mexican-American children. Turning to one of the parents present, he demanded, "Mrs. Perez isn't that what you told me?"

"Yes," Mrs. Perez replied, "because that was the only way I could get mine in this school, I heard. I want them to be where they would be the best and learn the most."

The board insisted that dividing the grades between the two buildings, as had been done in Westminster, would require extra teachers, for which there was no budget. Ross asserted just as strongly that there was no proof that extra teachers would be needed.

The board clung insistently to its refusal to desegregate. Judge

McCormick soon ordered the board to implement a plan to divide the two schools by grades: students in grades one through four would attend Roosevelt; those in grades five through eight would attend Lincoln. There was only minimal compliance with the order. It was clear that further action in El Modena would depend on the outcome of the appeal to the Ninth Circuit.

The Santa Ana school board also met in the fall of 1946 and declared its willingness to meet with community representatives to fashion an "amicable solution." It declined to dismantle the segregated schools but announced that it would permit some Mexican-American students to transfer, as long as they were "socially acceptable" and did not exceed the number of Anglo children seeking to transfer to another district. Like the El Modena board, the Santa Ana board would agree only to the most token reforms. Fred Ross and Hector Tarango were at that meeting, too. The LAO was also at the school board meetings, holding protests. It would soon transform itself into a League of United Latin American Citizens (LULAC) chapter and begin holding events to raise funds for the appeal.

Judge McCormick's decision, in fact, had a marked impact on local Mexican-American organizing efforts. There was already a Mexican-American Voters League in Orange County, but many of its members were unaware that LULAC existed. According to Alex Maldonado, a LULAC organizer named Floyd Apodaca was traveling through the county one day and decided that he needed a haircut. Apodaca found a local barbershop and, in the course of conversation, told the barber about LULAC. The barber then spoke with members of the Voters League, Frank Palomino and Alex Maldonado among them. Many of them were also members of the LAO, of which Tarango was a leader. The group held informal meetings in the barbershop and decided to create an Orange County chapter of LULAC. William H. Wheat, LULAC regional organizer for California, may have been involved as well. Fourteen of the men met in May 1946 to elect the new chapter's officers. Its first activity was raising money for the *Mendez* case. In November 1946 it organized "Mexico en Fantasia," a theatrical folklore performance, in the Santa Ana High School auditorium. Ignacio López, one of the plaintiffs in the San Bernardino swimming pool case and the editor of *El Espectador*, was the guest speaker. The following year the chapter raffled off a refrigerator and, later, held a sit-down dinner. LULAC members, along with other members of the Mexican-American community, knocked on families' doors, asking them to support the effort.

In nearby Ontario, Mexican-American protests led the town to desegregate its Grove School, in spite of a petition against integration signed by 1,400 Anglo parents. By September 1946, the Grove School had 177 Mexican-American and 155 non-Mexican-American students. Similar protests took place in Riverside, organized with the help of Ross and the newly created Bell Town Improvement League (Bell Town was a district in Riverside). The protests, coupled with the threat of a lawsuit that David Marcus was now prepared to bring on behalf of Riverside's Mexican-American and African-American children, resulted in the integration of schools in Bell Town. *La Opinión*, California's largest Spanish-language newspaper, which served Los Angeles and Southern California, reported in May 1946 that Mexican-American parents in Indio, California, had drawn on Judge McCormick's ruling to begin negotiations with the local school board to end segregation. Failing in that effort, they turned to a San Bernardino lawyer recommended by the Mexican consul in Los Angeles. The new tactic was more successful, and in September 1946 the district ended school segregation.

The two-year-old American Council on Race Relations had sent Fred Ross to Orange County to help expand a network of the grassroots Unity Leagues. The leagues worked on social issues and voting rights in addition to school matters. The excitement generated by *Mendez*, in addition to the new expectations fostered by the war and reflected in the creation of the leagues, encouraged organizing on a variety of issues. In Pomona, a group of fifty young Mexican-Americans, most of them World War II veterans, created a Unity League to help organize against discrimination and to push the candidacies of Mexican-Americans running for local office. Similar leagues sprang up in Chino, Ontario, San Bernardino, and Redlands, mobilizing the communities and electing a few Mexican-American officials.

The reaction in the legal community was just as notable. Requests for copies of the opinion poured into Judge McCormick's chambers from around the country. They came from lawyers as nearby as San Bernardino and as far away as St. Louis, Missouri; from the assistant attorney general of Texas, the New York City–based American Jewish Congress's Commission on Law and Social Action, the American Jewish Congress branch in Southern California, the ACLU of Northern California, and Fisk University, a historically black college. Each request was met with a polite note from the clerk of the court stating that the cost of a copy of the "Conclusions of Law" would be $4.75. A copy of the decision cost an additional 75 cents. George Sánchez wrote from Texas to ACLU executive cirector Roger Baldwin, based in New York City, "I hope that you have read the ruling on segregation of 'mexicans' of that Federal District Court in California. . . . I am having several hundred copies of this decision mimeographed for use by interested groups out here."

In New York, the NAACP's assistant special counsel Robert Carter, Thurgood Marshall's second in command and later a federal district court judge, expressed surprise that the NAACP had known nothing about the case. Marshall was in the Virgin Islands, recuperating from an illness, so Carter was effectively in charge. He immediately understood that if the case reached the Supreme Court, it could be the one to attack segregated education on its face. He had come to believe that sociological evidence, illustrating the psychological and pedagogical effects of school segregation, could be a useful weapon in the litigation arsenal. Other lawyers who worked with the NAACP were less sanguine. The social sciences, they said, were not pure science, so their findings were too weak to use in court. Carter knew, however, that as long as he was prepared to stand up to the other attorneys, Marshall would support him. The *Mendez* case was too good an opportunity to ignore, and Carter began drafting a brief. The NAACP would enter the case at the appeals level as an amicus.

So would the American Jewish Congress (AJC), the Japanese-American Citizens League (JACL), and the national office of the ACLU. Carter was a member of the ACLU, as were some of the other lawyers coming into the case, and the NAACP, ACLU, National Lawyers Guild, and AJC were used to working together. The legal talent now connected to the case was extraordinary. Among those signing the ACLU–National Lawyers Guild brief were Arthur Garfield Hays, Osmond K. Fraenkel, and Julien Cornell. Hays was a founding member of the ACLU, its general counsel for decades, and one of the nation's great civil liberties litigators. Fraenkel, a member of the ACLU's Board of Directors, would succeed Hays as general counsel.

Cornell, a Quaker, had represented conscientious objectors during World War II. A. L. Wirin was named on the ACLU–National Lawyers Guild brief both as a participant in the ACLU effort and as being "of counsel" for the JACL. As noted earlier, he had been one of the attorneys in the Sleepy Lagoon case and had represented the ACLU's Southern California branch throughout the *Mendez* trial. The name of Fred Okrand, also of the ACLU branch, appeared next to Wirin's. The other name on the brief, listed as "of counsel" for the JACL, was Saburo Kido, its president. He, along with Wirin and Okrand, had filed an amicus brief in the *Korematsu* relocation case. Charles Christopher again represented the Los Angeles chapter of the National Lawyers Guild.

A number of distinguished attorneys signed the AJC's brief. Much of it was written by Alexander H. Pekelis, a brilliant former jurisprudence professor from Europe. Because he had not been admitted to the bar in the United States, however, Pekelis was listed on the brief only as "Special Advisor." He and Will Maslow, the AJC's general counsel and future executive director, who worked on the brief, had just helped create the organization's litigation entity—the Commission on Law and Social Action—modeled on the ACLU and NAACP. Pauli Murray, listed second on the brief, was an attorney who had helped create the Congress of Racial Equality in 1942. She would become the nation's first female African-American Episcopal priest as well as a founder of the National Organization for Women. Carey McWilliams was also listed on the AJC brief. Some of these lawyers would add their names to amicus briefs when the NAACP took the case of *Brown v. Board of Education* to the U.S. Supreme Court.

The NAACP's own brief in *Mendez* was written primarily by Robert Carter, with some input from Loren Miller, the only attorney on the brief who was admitted to practice in California. Miller was an African-American journalist and attorney with expertise in cases involving restrictive covenants (contracts preventing white home owners from selling to people of other races). He would later become a California state judge. The first name on the NAACP's brief was Thurgood Marshall, although Marshall's illness prevented him from having much to do with the case beyond looking over Carter's first draft.

The main briefs, however, were those submitted by Marcus and

Holden. Marcus added attorney William Strong to his brief, probably to help with the legal research required to bolster his arguments with citations of relevant cases. Ogle's name appeared first on the county's brief, but as at the trial court level, it was Holden who did the bulk of the work. Royal E. Hubbard, another Orange County deputy counsel, was brought in as well. There were no amicus briefs on their side.

Both parties' briefs repeated their arguments before the district court, so they need not be detailed here. Holden had decided that his best argument was the jurisdictional one: that because education was a state matter, the case did not belong in federal court. In addition, Supreme Court decisions in cases such as *Plessy* made it clear that segregated education was constitutional as long as the education offered to all students was equal. Marcus wrote extensively on the question of jurisdiction and insisted that the school districts' acts constituted the kind of state action that was prohibited by the Fourteenth Amendment.

It is not uncommon for organizations coming into a case as amici to divide up the work, each emphasizing a different facet of the case, and they did so in *Mendez*. The national ACLU and the Los Angeles chapter of the National Lawyers Guild, filing a joint brief with the JACL, addressed the question of jurisdiction. The Fourteenth Amendment had been violated, they said, because "the evidence was overwhelming that the real reason for the segregation was the unscientific and un-American theory of the supposed inferiority of the children of Mexican descent." The students had been denied the equal protection of the laws because they were discriminated against in the absence of "a reasonable distinction." The experience of the war was much on the minds of the attorneys. "During the trial, defendants, to their shame, contended that children of Mexican descent were inferior to other children," they wrote. "If appellants can justify discrimination on the basis of ancestry only, then who can tell what minority group will be next on the road to persecution. If we learned one lesson from the horrors of Nazism, it is that no minority group, and in fact, no person is safe, once the State . . . can arbitrarily discriminate against any person or group."

The NAACP brief was very much a reflection of Carter's thinking. "I used it as a trial run for *Brown*," he said later, referring to *Brown v. Board of Education*. Carter told an Illinois law student writing an article about the case that he expected *Mendez* to reach the Supreme Court. That court, he believed, would ignore the argument about the unconstitutionality of segregation and decide that the segregation of Mexican-American students was a violation of California law. As Thurgood Marshall had written to Carl Murphy, the NAACP did not think the time was ripe to challenge segregation as such. Nonetheless, Carter was thinking ahead, and *Mendez* presented him with an opportunity to shape his thoughts.

He did so in spite of the fact that Marcus, with *Plessy* and its progeny in mind, had emphasized in his own brief what he clearly felt was a crucial argument: "*It should be noted, as all parties agreed below, that no question of race discrimination is involved in this case*, since persons of Latin and Mexican extraction are members of the 'white' race." The NAACP brief was therefore somewhat curious in context, because its argument had everything to do with race and focused primarily on African-Americans, with Mexican-Americans a seeming afterthought. The brief began with an assertion that the Fourteenth Amendment was designed to outlaw "classifications and discrimination on the basis of race." "Segregation on a racial basis in the public school system," it added, "is a type of arbitrary and unreasonable discrimination which should be forbidden under our laws." That was followed by statistical information about the segregation of African-American students throughout the South, including the difference in dollar amounts spent on white and African-American schools. There was no mention of the differential between Mexican-American and Anglo schools. One consequence of such segregation, the brief continued, was "to deprive the Negro community of the professional services it desperately needs," and the small number of black doctors and lawyers in the nation was evidence of that. But "one of the most important inequities of all" was the creation within "the minority citizen" — and here, mention was also made of Mexicans, Latin Americans, and Japanese — of "a feeling of 'second-class citizenship.' " Segregation "promotes racial strife by teaching the children of both the dominant and minority groups to regard each other as something different and apart."

In addition, Carter wrote, there was nothing to keep a federal court from declaring that segregation in a public school system was unconstitutional. *Plessy* dealt only with railroad cars, not with education, and a line of cases decided since *Plessy* indicated that the Court was moving

136   { *Chapter 8* }

toward a holding that "classifications and distinctions on the basis of race [are] contrary to our fundamental law." The conclusion: "It is clear, therefore, that segregation in our public schools must be invalidated as violative of the Constitution and laws of the United States." The appeals court would refer to this argument in its decision—but not favorably.

The brief submitted by the AJC referred to it as well. Though generated by *Mendez*, the AJC brief stated that it agreed with the NAACP's argument and went on to present an eloquent thirty-five-page indictment of all segregation and an analysis of the relationship between societal prejudice and legally sanctioned segregation. It began by arguing that "mere identity of physical facilities" is not the same thing as equality in the economic, political, or legal sense. Here it turned to the recent example of Nazi Germany:

If the Nazis while proclaiming the essential inferiority of the "Jewish race," compelled Jews to wear clothes of one given color while reserving another to the master race, it could not be said that Jews have received equal clothing facilities even if the physical qualities of the clothing were identical to those given to the members of the Aryan race.

The same was true of public facilities:

The official assignment to a group of separate parks, schools or halls based on an officially stated conviction of the group's inferiority would be an assignment of facilities inferior per se, regardless of their physical identity with the facilities assigned to the "better" group.

Superintendent Kent had testified about the supposed inferiority of Mexican-Americans, the brief continued. His ideas reflected their social inequality and a popular belief in their inferiority. "Whenever law" or, as here, action by state officials "adopts a social classification based on a notion of inferiority," however, "it transforms the pre-existing *social* inequality into *legal* inequality." This, in turn, will "intensify and deepen the social inequality from which it stems" because "law is, indeed, at the same time the consequence and the cause of social phenomena. . . . When a more or less inarticulate social feeling of racial superiority is clothed with the dignity of an official law, that feeling acquires a concreteness and assertiveness which it did not possess before. . . . An official action, born in and based on a discriminatory classification, breeds in turn more inequality and more prejudice." The "undeniable effect of classification by race, color or ethnic origin" is "to enforce an inferior economic and social status upon the non-white minority." Such legally sanctioned inferiority ran counter to the mandates of the Constitution, and when it occurred, the courts had an obligation to intervene "for the protection of the basic values of our society."

This is particularly true in the area of education, the brief continued, paralleling the thinking of the experts who had testified at the trial. "The value and the desirability of an educational institution is particularly dependent on intangible elements," the AJC asserted. "The physical characteristics of the benches and desks of a school shrink into utter insignificance when compared with the social and psychological environment which the school offers to its children." That "social and psychological environment" could be devastating. Children who were "deemed superior are often, in manifesting their innocent pride, more cruel than normal adults usually are. On the other side, children who feel that they are treated as inferior are more bitterly humiliated by the social stigma that strikes them than adults can be." They are likely to suffer the "deepest and most lasting social and psychological evil results." Segregation based on assumptions of inferiority "perpetuate[s] racial prejudice and contributes to the degradation and humiliation of the minority children." The brief then cited a host of articles and books documenting the psychological effects of segregation and suggesting its impact on learning. In this, it foreshadowed the argument made by the NAACP in *Brown v. Board of Education* and reflected a similar reliance on the findings of social scientists.

The AJC brief went at the *Plessy* "separate but equal" doctrine from a different angle, challenging its conclusion on factual rather than legal grounds. *Plessy*, Pekelis wrote, took it as fact that segregated railroad cars did not imply racial inferiority. Now, however, social science had shown that "fact" to be incorrect and that segregation did connote inferiority. The facts therefore required the courts to strike down segregation.

The AJC brief also turned to international law—a daring and innovative step in 1946, when nations had barely begun to take international human rights law seriously. The United States had ratified the Charter of the United Nations in July 1945, and the brief contended that ratification made "the abolition of discrimination on account of race, creed, [and] color . . . a part of national policy." The brief suggested that eliminating discrimination was necessary if the nation wanted to remain a citizen in good standing of the international order, for the charter represented the belief "that human rights are a matter of international concern, that individual freedom and international peace are inseparable, that a world in which racial hatred, contempt, discrimination, segregation or other forms of interracial and intergroup humiliation continue to exist within the various nations is a world in which there can be no lasting peace among nations. In other words," the brief noted in a striking analogy, "what the United Nations did was not unlike the adoption of an International Fourteenth Amendment."

There was one final point: equality was not something that benefited only minorities. "We are convinced that the treatment of minorities in a community is indicative of its political and moral standards and ultimately determinative of the happiness of all its members. In arguing here in favor of the rights of one ethnic group we are certain to serve the interests of all Americans." The country was an amalgam of immigrants. How were they to be melded into one nation? "One of the answers . . . is the existence of a school where children from heterogeneous backgrounds come together, study, live and work together and acquire in the formative years of their lives that mutual understanding and respect without which the existence of a free country is inconceivable." Clearly thinking not only of Mexican-American students but also of others, such as eastern European Jews, who arrived in the United States by boat during the first half of the twentieth century, the brief asserted that schools "in which children less far removed from the steerage of an immigrant ship, children with a foreign language background, are segregated by State action from children of the Anglo-Saxon, English speaking group" were counterproductive. They were as cruel as they were unconstitutional. The humiliation of children, the brief concluded, was particularly vicious. "Their humiliation strikes at the very roots of the American Commonwealth. Their humiliation threatens the more perfect union which the Constitution seeks to achieve."

Robert W. Kenny, the attorney general of California, submitted a brief of his own, telling the court that he was "in full accord" with the briefs filed by the AJC as well as those written by Marcus and the NAACP. He would leave the Fourteenth Amendment question to the parties and the other amici and focus instead on the laws of California. The school districts had violated those laws, he wrote, because the California Education Code permitted segregation only of Indian and Asian children. Kenny's argument was not surprising, because the state law was quite clear. What was surprising was that he went on to condemn all school segregation. "We in California like to think of our people as enlightened and free from prejudice . . . we are convinced that the great majority of Californians want no part of race discrimination or segregation. The Attorney General is convinced that segregation of pupils on account of race is not the policy of the State." It *was* the policy of the state, of course, but the attorney general was signaling that he thought it should be changed. Moreover, it was highly unlikely that he would have done so without the acquiescence or at least the knowledge of Earl Warren, who was then the governor of the state. Kenny had been elected attorney general in 1942, the same year Warren won the governorship. Before that, Kenny had been a founding member of the National Lawyers Guild, a state judge, and a state legislator. His thinking about segregation clearly paralleled that of the other amici attorneys; in fact, he was very much a part of their intellectual circle.

The consequences of Kenny's view and, by extension, Warren's would be seen after the appeals court handed down its decision. Before that happened, however, Marcus and Holden had to present their arguments verbally before the seven Ninth Circuit judges in their San Francisco courthouse.

CHAPTER 9

From the Court of Appeals
to the State Legislature

The seven judges of the Ninth Circuit Court of Appeals looked out at a packed courtroom on the morning of December 9, 1946. *Mendez* was finally attracting national attention — even the *New York Times* had sent a reporter — and extra seats had to be brought to the courtroom for all the people who crowded in. "El Caso de Segregación en Orange County Toma Proporciones Nacionales" (Orange County Segregation Case Captures National Attention), *El Espectador* trumpeted on November 15. The case, the *San Francisco Chronicle* reported on December 10, was generally seen "as one of the most important ever to come under Federal jurisdiction in this area."

Six of the seven judges who listened to the attorneys that day had been appointed to the court by President Franklin D. Roosevelt; one, by President Harry S. Truman. Roosevelt had made a point of bringing minority group members into his political coalition, and he had created the Committee on Fair Employment Practices that had heartened Mexican-Americans. It was reasonable to speculate that his West Coast appointees might be sympathetic to claims of racial and ethnic prejudice. Judge Albert Lee Stephens, one of the Roosevelt appointees, was a graduate of the University of Southern California Law School. He had practiced law privately and had also served as a justice of the peace, California civil service commissioner, Los Angeles city attorney, and judge of the California Court of Appeals before being appointed to the federal bench. He had the kind of colorful prejudicial background that was far from unusual in California in the first half of the twentieth century: at various times he had been a butcher wagon driver, gold mine security guard, and bicycle salesman. Stephens, as it turned out, would write the opinion for the court in *Mendez*.

Judge William Denman, sitting not far from Stephens, was a well-connected and equally colorful California figure. One of his ancestors had been among the first Europeans to settle in America in 1631, and his father had been president of the San Francisco Board of Education. Denman himself had graduated from Harvard Law School, but before entering the University of California at Berkeley in 1890, he punched cattle for a year. In 1906, as a great earthquake and fire raged through San Francisco and many families were left homeless, he used a pistol to force teams into service so that they could move food from the docks to the refugee camps. His civic activities as a lawyer included campaigning for the nonpartisan election of judges and investigating municipal corruption in San Francisco. Denman, who would also write an opinion, had made his strongly negative feelings about discrimination clear when he dissented from his court's decision in the *Korematsu* case.

The *Mendez* attorneys' statements were familiar to anyone who had followed the case. Ogle and Holden claimed that federal courts had no jurisdiction over the matter. As the U.S. Supreme Court had repeatedly held, they also argued, "segregation of itself alone is not denial of equal protection of the laws." Provision of equal facilities satisfied the demands of the Fourteenth Amendment. Marcus replied that because Latinos were Caucasian, the case did not involve racial discrimination, and the Supreme Court's segregation decisions were irrelevant. He emphasized ethnic differences, however, and tacitly reminded the court of the horrors of Nazi Germany. "If we accept the premise as laid down by the other side that a school board can do anything it desires and not be in violation of the Federal Constitution," he told the judges, "a board can start segregation with children of Mexican descent, go on with Germans and other national origins and end by dividing with respect to religion, and we'll have the same situation we had in Germany." The school boards segregated on the basis of names that suggested Mexican descent, he added. Judge Denman commented that he had once known a Guatemalan man who was seven-eighths Spanish but whose name was O'Shaughnessy. Would he be segregated in Orange County? Yes, Marcus replied, because "they also segregate by appearance as well as names."

After the hearing ended, there was once again nothing to do but wait, and this time, people outside California were waiting as well. Lawrence E. Davies, the *New York Times* reporter who covered the proceedings, wrote on December 21 that the case was being "closely watched as a guinea-pig." In March 1947 the *Nation* magazine published an article by Carey McWilliams entitled "Is Your Name Gonzales?" Unless the districts appealed from what McWilliams assumed would be an adverse decision by the Ninth Circuit, he predicted, the case would make "judicial and social history."

The California state legislature was also watching. In January 1947 four members of the assembly introduced a bill to end segregated education in the state by repealing the laws permitting the segregation of Indian and Asian children. One of the four was Augustus Hawkins, who would become the first African-American from California to serve in the U.S. House of Representatives and a founder of the Congressional Black Caucus. The assembly passed the bill on April 10, which, as it turned out, was only four days before the *Mendez* decision was handed down by a unanimous court on April 14.

The opinion written for the court by Judge Stephens was far less pathbreaking than Judge McCormick's, but he too began by dismissing Orange County's jurisdictional claim. He cited a variety of U.S. Supreme Court decisions holding that officials who act in accordance with the authority bestowed on them by the state are acting as agents of the state, whether or not their actions are legitimate. The segregation imposed by the school boards was state action and was subject to the Fourteenth Amendment's requirement that states treat all people equally. Federal law gave federal courts jurisdiction over Fourteenth Amendment claims.

Judge Stephens rejected the county's argument that the Supreme Court's segregation decisions were controlling. His reason was nonetheless quite different from Marcus's. Those decisions, Stephens wrote, were handed down in cases where the state legislature had mandated segregation. That was not the situation here. "Nowhere in any California law is there a suggestion that any segregation can be made of children within one of the great races," Stephens noted (although he declared in a footnote that he found the current scholarly division of people into the Caucasoid, Mongoloid, and Negroid races to be unsatisfactory). Whatever race Mexican-Americans belonged to, they were neither American Indians nor Asians, and those were the only categories of children that California law permitted to be segregated. Stephens was willing to concede that California could enact a law permitting the segregation of Mexican-Americans, but it had not done so, which meant that the school boards had deprived the plaintiff children of liberty and property without due process and equal protection of the laws.

Stephens could have stopped there, and perhaps the first draft of his opinion did so. As we will see, however, Judge Denman wrote a concurrence that challenged the basis for Stephens's holding, and Stephens apparently felt obligated to reply to it. He assertively declined to emulate Judge McCormick and tackle the question of segregation head-on. "There is argument in two of the amicus curiae briefs that we should strike out independently on the whole question of segregation," he noted, "on the ground that recent world stirring events have set men to the reexamination of concepts considered fixed. Of course, judges as well as all others must keep abreast of the times but judges must ever be on their guard lest they rationalize outright legislation under the too free use of the power to interpret. We are not tempted by the siren who calls to us that the sometimes slow and tedious ways of democratic legislation [are] no longer respected in a progressive society." In other words, if any institution was to end segregation, it would have to be the elected legislature rather than a panel of appointed judges. The decision would stand on the basis of the school districts' having violated California law and would say nothing about the validity of segregation or of segregated education as such — one of the reasons the case would have far less impact than *Brown v. Board of Education*. Stephens nonetheless gave an unusual nod to Judge McCormick, writing in a footnote, "The author of this opinion deems it appropriate to note that the case was tried to the distinguished Senior Judge of the Southern District of California, Honorable Paul J. McCormick." Ironically, in order to overturn a regulation that was clearly based on race, McCormick had to circumvent legal precedents by saying that the case was not about race. Stephens, too, denied that the case was about race. He decided the case only on the basis of California law.

Judge Denman was having no part of Stephens's timidity, which was why he wrote a concurrence of his own. In it, he chided the court for not citing *Lopez v. Seccombe*, the San Bernardino swimming pool case, which he described as the kind of blow against discrimination he would have preferred for the Ninth Circuit to strike in *Mendez*. If the "vicious principle" that Orange and San Bernardino counties sought to establish was followed elsewhere, Denman warned, it could be applied to American Italians, Armenians, Greeks, Dalmatians, and Jews, emulating Hitler. Such segregation would "infect" the minds of American children.

Denman lashed out at the school boards. "What is overlooked in the court's opinion is the fact that the appellants themselves declare they have violated their oaths of office and, in effect, say, 'Well what are you going to do about it?'" he chided. "It is to such school officials, who so violate their oaths of office and openly break both the state and federal laws and who set such an example to the boys and girls, that these adolescents are entrusted to grow up in the American way of life." He urged the relevant "prosecuting authorities" and grand juries of Southern California to take note of what he clearly viewed as criminal behavior by the conspiring school boards. Dismissing the fiction that the "Mexican" and "Anglo" schools were in fact equal, Denman maintained that the school districts "clearly fail even to give equal facilities to the children in the two classes of schools."

None of the other judges signed on to Denman's opinion, either because they were reluctant to tackle the question of segregation or because they found his language too inflammatory. In any event, it was Stephens's moderation rather than Denman's outrage that made new law in California. The question of whether segregation was constitutionally permissible was left to be addressed in some other forum. The Ninth Circuit was willing to say only that Mexican-American children could not be segregated because the legislature had not decided that sending them to separate schools was state policy. The districts would have to desegregate or carry their appeal to the U.S. Supreme Court—or they could turn to the California state legislature, which could add Mexican-Americans to the segregation law. They chose not to pursue the case, perhaps because the legislature was already in the process of making it clear that the Orange County districts were out of step with the times.

Governor Earl Warren agreed with that assessment. Drew Pearson was a well-known journalist who wrote the influential "Washington Merry-Go-Round" column. According to Pearson's column of May

11, 1947, Judge Denman had sent a letter to the governor after the *Mendez* decision was handed down, saying that the rulings in the San Bernardino swimming pool case and *Mendez* meant that the segregation of Mexican-Americans should be ended throughout California. If it were not, Denman continued, the ambassadors of twenty Latin American nations would technically be excluded from California parks. Warren, in turn, wrote to Senator Herbert W. Slater, chairman of the California senate's education committee, stating, "I personally do not see how we can carry out the spirit of the United Nations if we deny fundamental rights to our Latin American neighbors." Denman and Warren obviously were aware of the international implications of American segregation laws. So, perhaps, was the California legislature. The California senate passed the antisegregation bill on June 3. On June 5 the Santa Ana board voted to inform Joel Ogle that it wanted him to drop the litigation. Nine days later, on June 14, Warren signed the antisegregation bill into law. Because the school districts did not appeal the Ninth Circuit's decision to the U.S. Supreme Court, and because the case had been decided by the circuit court on the basis of California law rather than the Fourteenth Amendment, the case carried legal weight only in California.

It had a substantial impact nonetheless. The country's legal elite — at least the part of it outside the South — was clearly in agreement with Judge Denman, the state legislature, and Governor Warren. Northern and western law reviews saw Judge McCormick's decision as the writing on the wall. His opinion, the *Yale Law Journal* wrote in June 1947, "has questioned the basic assumption of the *Plessy* case and may portend a complete reversal of the doctrine." Drawing on statistics in the NAACP's brief, the *Journal* declared that the facts that 34.5 percent of African-Americans had failed to meet the 1943 minimum educational standards for military service, and that there were too few African-American physicians, dentists, and lawyers, indicated that segregated education was counterproductive. "The only barrier to a flat holding that segregation is a denial of 'equal protection of the laws' is, in the last analysis, the *Plessy* case," the article continued. "However, the basic assumption of the Court in that case, that compulsory segregation does not imply social inferiority, has become untenable in the light of our knowledge of psychology and sociology. . . . It is to be hoped" that the Supreme Court would overrule *Plessy*. The *Michigan*

Law Review called the *Mendez* decision "a radical departure from the tacit assumption of the legality of racial segregation" and predicted that it, in concert with the higher education cases the NAACP had won in the Supreme Court, "may well force a reconsideration of the whole problem." The *Columbia Law Review* urged the Supreme Court to overturn *Plessy*, agreeing that "modern sociological investigation would appear to have conclusively demonstrated" that segregation implies inferiority. The *Southern California Law Review* called segregated education "anomalous" in "a nation priding itself on its solid foundation of basic tolerance and equality of opportunity."

Phylon, published by the historically black Clark Atlanta University, was one of the few journals that had written about the district court decision in 1946. Its 1949 issue contained a summary of the court of appeals decision and added, "It would appear highly desirable to secure a review by our highest tribunal of the suggestions set forth by the two courts in the Westminster case."

La Opinión read the court of appeals decision as affirming that students of Latin descent were members of the white race and as tying American segregationists to Hitler's anti-Semitic theories. *El Espectador* also gave the decision front-page coverage and reproduced much of Pearson's column about the Denman and Warren letters. Robert Carter was also excited about the case. "This case brings the American courts closer to a decision on the whole question of segregation," he wrote in a memorandum to the NAACP's public relations department.

The school districts, of course, were far less pleased, but they more or less complied with the ruling. Westminster, as noted earlier, had desegregated even before the Ninth Circuit's decision. The Santa Ana board decided to permit Mexican-American children to transfer for the 1947–1948 school year, and when the schools opened in September, 50 percent of the students at the formerly Anglo Franklin School were Mexican-Americans. The board in Garden Grove bused some Anglo students to Hoover. El Modena allowed some Mexican-American children to attend the Anglo Roosevelt School and gradually moved all kindergarten through grade three pupils to the Lincoln School and those in the upper grades to Roosevelt.

The success of *Mendez* both fit into and encouraged a spate of organizing and litigation. Mexican-American parents in El Modena came together under the auspices of the Latin American League after the Ninth Circuit ruled, and in the May 1947 school board election, they managed to replace a pro-segregation school board member with another, less biased Anglo. Anglo parents in El Modena, however, continued to resist desegregation. Many transferred their children to other districts; later, they managed to have part of the district itself transferred to the nearby, all-white Tustin district. In June 1947 the board renewed Superintendent Hammarsten's contract for four years. The Mexican-American community continued to organize, and in 1948 Jésus Martinez was elected to the El Modena board, becoming its first Mexican-American member. When Alex Lievanos ran for the board in 1950, however, he was beaten by an Anglo candidate. In 1951, after Hammarsten made a number of racist comments, the Mexican-American parents petitioned the board not to renew his contract. The two Anglo members of the three-member board ignored the parents and Martinez's objections, voting not only to rehire Hammarsten but to raise his salary as well. Martinez chose not to run for reelection, and Primo Rodriguez was elected without opposition to fill his seat. The victory was somewhat hollow, however, as all the elementary schools in Orange County were reorganized into one Anglo-controlled district in 1953.

Mendez nonetheless continued to send out ripples. In 1948 Alfred V. Aguirre, a World War II veteran, organized the Veterans and Citizens of Placentia (a town in northern Orange County). The new group quickly registered more than 300 Placentia citizens to vote. Aguirre and his siblings had all been bused to the local "Mexican" school, and they and many other Mexican-American residents were determined not to let that happen to their children. They had learned about the *Mendez* case, and so, after petitioning the school board unsuccessfully, Aguirre and another member of the group consulted attorney G. W. Marshall about possible litigation. Marshall advised them that although a lawsuit certainly would succeed, given the holding in *Mendez*, they should try petitioning the school board one more time before following the expensive litigation route. The board, now faced with the threat of a court case, opened the "Anglo" Bradford Elementary School to all children. A year later there were so few students in the "Mexican" school that it closed. One of the new students at Bradford was Aguirre's son Frederick, who later became a California judge and wrote the article about *Mendez* discussed later in this chapter. A year after *Mendez* was decided, scholar Mary Peters surveyed 100 nonurban school districts in Southern and central California. Seventy-eight percent of the districts that responded had segregated Mexican-American students in the recent past; only 18 percent still did so.

Ninth Circuit rulings do not control the law in Texas, which is part of the Fifth Circuit. Nonetheless, Gustavo (Gus) C. García, an attorney and activist, asked Texas attorney general Price Daniel whether *Mendez* meant that segregation on the basis of national origin was illegal. Daniel replied that it did, but students could still be segregated on the basis of language deficiency. Since *Mendez* did nothing to change existing practices in Texas, García and LULAC filed suit against four south Texas school districts in June 1948 on behalf of Mexican-American children and their parents. Like Marcus, García and his team brought expert witnesses to testify about the negative effects of segregation and asserted that "separate but equal" could never be equal; as in *Mendez*, the attorneys argued that the Supreme Court's racial segregation decisions were irrelevant because Mexican-Americans were white. Judge Ben C. Rice of the federal district court in the Western District of Texas agreed that segregation of Mexican-Americans was not authorized by Texas law and violated the equal protection clause. His decision in *Delgado v. Bastrop Independent School District*, however, did permit separate first-grade classes for language-deficient students who were identified as such by "scientifically standardized" tests. The Texas superintendent of public instruction advised school officials that if districts wished to separate first-graders on the basis of language proficiency, all the children were to be given the Inter-American Test in Oral English. Most districts simply ignored the directive.

Clearly, the prejudices that led to segregated schools were not going to disappear quickly; equally clearly, the fight was going to continue. It did so with the continued cooperation of many of the lawyers and organizations involved in *Mendez*. In 1948 scholar-activist George I. Sánchez used a LULAC fund to hire A. L. Wirin as one of García's co-counsels in the *Delgado* case. After the court decision in *Delgado*, Thurgood Marshall called Wirin and asked for the affidavits of the expert witnesses and other documents in the case so the NAACP could draw on the *Delgado* lawyers' experience. In 1950 Wirin brought *Gonzalez v. Sheely*, a Mexican-American school desegregation case in Arizona, and asked Sánchez to testify as an expert witness. (Judge Dave W. Ling, ruling for the plaintiffs in *Gonzalez* in 1951, quoted extensively from Judge McCormick's decision.) Sánchez had been corresponding with the ACLU's Roger Baldwin about possible school desegregation litigation in Texas. In response, Baldwin created the ACLU's Robert Marshall Civil Liberties Trust to fund litigation on behalf of Latinos in the Southwest. In 1951 he turned the funding of block grants through the trust over to Sánchez, who used much of the money for Mexican-American civil rights efforts in the Southwest. Mexican-Americans had become part of the loose coalition of civil rights attorneys and organizations that litigated against segregation and discrimination.

The American GI Forum (AGIF), one of many Mexican-American organizations created after World War II, also participated in the *Delgado* case. AGIF was founded in 1948, largely at the behest of Hector P. García, a Texas physician and veteran, with help from Gus García. Although it was concerned with obtaining equal health, education, and pension benefits for Mexican-American veterans, its goals included encouraging Mexican-American students and fostering desegregation. AGIF and LULAC continued to litigate against segregation in Texas throughout the 1950s.

Simultaneously, the NAACP maintained its campaign of bringing cases designed to end segregation on the university level, and it achieved success after success in the Supreme Court. In 1950 the Court unanimously struck down Texas's attempt to confine African-American law students to a hastily constructed "law school for Negroes" rather than admit them to the University of Texas Law School (*Sweatt v. Painter*), as well as the University of Oklahoma's policy of confining its only African-American Ph.D. candidate in education to separate spaces in its graduate school (*McLaurin v. Oklahoma State Regents*). The cases were argued by Thurgood Marshall and Robert Carter, along with other NAACP attorneys. By that time, many of the nation's legal elite had moved beyond a conversation about segregation and were supporting efforts to overturn it. Notably, it was not only the ACLU and the JACL that submitted amicus briefs in *McLaurin*. The U.S. Department of Justice also came in on McLaurin's side — yet another indication of the changing times.

The NAACP decided in the early 1950s that the moment was finally ripe for a frontal attack on segregation at the elementary school level. The cases it brought, which culminated in *Brown v. Board of Education*, did not involve Mexican-Americans. They were connected to *Mendez* nonetheless. As Robert Carter said repeatedly, the NAACP's brief in *Mendez* was its trial run for *Brown*: it was, as noted, a brief in which the organization both attacked segregation as such and relied on the findings of social scientists to bolster its case. The brief the NAACP submitted in *Brown* included a twenty-four-page appendix entitled "The Effects of Segregation and the Consequences of Desegregation: A Social Science Statement." Thurgood Marshall asked David Marcus to travel to New York to help as the NAACP was preparing *Brown*. Marcus, who disliked traveling and was reluctant to leave his single-practitioner law practice, declined, but he did send Marshall his case notes.

By the time *Brown* reached the Supreme Court, Earl Warren was no longer the governor of California. He was the nation's chief justice, and it was he who delivered the Supreme Court's unanimous decision in *Brown*. Judge Frederick Aguirre, in the article "*Mendez v Westminster School District*: How It Affected *Brown v Board of Education*," has pointed out some of the striking similarities between McCormick's decision in *Mendez* and Warren's opinion in *Brown*.

Mendez: "Commingling of the entire student body instills and develops a common cultural attitude among the school children which is imperative for the perpetuation of American institutions and ideals."

Brown: "It [education] is required in the performance of our most basic public responsibilities, even service in the armed forces. It is the very foundation of good citizenship. Today, it is a principal instrument in awakening the child to cultural values."

Mendez: "The evidence clearly shows that Spanish-speaking children are retarded in learning English by lack of exposure to its use because of segregation."

Brown: "Segregation with the sanction of law therefore has a tendency to retard the educational and mental development of

Negro children and to deprive them of some of the benefits they would receive in a racially integrated school system."

Mendez: "It is also established by the record that the methods of segregation prevalent in the defendant school districts foster antagonisms in the children and suggest inferiority among them where none exists."

Brown: "Segregation of white and colored children in public schools has a detrimental effect upon the colored children. The impact is greater when it has the sanction of the law; for the policy of separating the races is usually interpreted as denoting the inferiority of the Negro group."

Mendez: "The 'equal protection of the laws' pertaining to the public school system in California is not provided by furnishing in separate schools the same technical facilities, text books and courses of instruction to children of Mexican ancestry that are available to the other public school children regardless of their ancestry."

Brown: "We conclude that in the field of public education the doctrine of 'separate but equal' has no place. Separate education facilities are inherently unequal. Therefore, we hold that the plaintiffs . . . are deprived of the equal protection of the laws."

Mendez: "A paramount requisite in the American system of public education is social equality. It must be open to all children by unified school association regardless of lineage."

Brown: "In these days, it is doubtful that any child may reasonably be expected to succeed in life if he is denied the opportunity of an education. Such an opportunity, where the state has undertaken to provide it, is a right which must be made available to all on equal terms."

There is no hard evidence that Warren was directly affected by McCormick's opinion, and Warren did not cite *Mendez* in *Brown*. However, Governor Warren's attorney general submitted an amicus brief in *Mendez*, and Warren and the California legislature changed the state segregation law shortly thereafter, suggesting that the governor was at least familiar with the gist of the opinion. Ed Cray, one of Warren's biographers, wrote that, as governor, Warren "aligned the state against an Orange County school district that sought to assign

Hispanic pupils to separate grammar schools," indicating Warren's involvement in the decision to enter the case at the appeals court level.

The connection between discrimination against Mexican-Americans and discrimination against African-Americans was in fact made explicit by Warren not long before the Supreme Court handed down its decision in *Brown*, when it announced its holding in the case of *Hernandez v. Texas*. Pete Hernández had been convicted of murder by a Texas jury from which Mexican-Americans were excluded. His lawyers appealed to the Texas Court of Criminal Appeals, arguing that the all-Anglo jury violated Hernández's right, as a member of a "class" (group of people), to the equal protection of the laws mandated by the Fourteenth Amendment. The Texas court held that because Mexicans were "white," they did not constitute a separate class protected by the Fourteenth Amendment. As "whites" had not been excluded from the jury, Hernández had been properly tried by a jury of his peers.

After hearing the first Mexican-American lawyers — including Gus García — ever to argue before it, a unanimous Supreme Court disagreed. The Supreme Court is meticulous about ending attorneys' oral arguments when their allotted time has expired, indicated by a flashing red light at the attorneys' rostrum. In fact, there are jokes about chief justices cutting lawyers off in the middle of the word *of*. In January 1954 Chief Justice Warren nonetheless signaled his interest in the case by allowing García to continue his presentation after the red light indicated that his time had expired. Four months later, Warren announced the Court's decision in *Hernandez v. Texas*. "The State of Texas would have us hold that there are only two classes — white and Negro — within the contemplation of the Fourteenth Amendment," he stated. He went on to rule, as Marcus had argued in *Mendez*, that the Fourteenth Amendment protects Mexican-Americans as well. In doing so, he offered a mini-lesson in the history of American racism:

> Throughout our history differences in race and color have defined easily identifiable groups which have at times required the aid of the courts in securing equal treatment under the laws. But community prejudices are not static, and from time to time other differences from the community norm may define other groups which need the same protection. Whether such a group exists within a community is a question of fact. When the existence of a distinct

class is demonstrated, and it is further shown that the laws, as written or as applied, single out that class for different treatment not based on some reasonable classification, the guarantees of the Constitution have been violated. The Fourteenth Amendment is not directed solely against discrimination due to a "two-class theory" — that is, based upon differences between "white" and Negro. . . . The exclusion of otherwise eligible persons from jury service solely because of their ancestry or national origin is discrimination prohibited by the Fourteenth Amendment.

The chief justice then turned to the situation as it existed in Jackson County, where *Hernandez* was tried. It was all too similar to the situation Gonzalo Méndez had encountered in Orange County.

The participation of persons of Mexican descent in business and community groups was shown to be slight. Until very recent times, children of Mexican descent were required to attend a segregated school for the first four grades. At least one restaurant in town prominently displayed a sign announcing "No Mexicans Served." On the courthouse grounds at the time of the hearing, there were two men's toilets, one unmarked, and the other marked "Colored Men" and "Hombres Aqui" ("Men Here").

The decision was handed down on May 3, 1954, two weeks before the Court decided *Brown v. Board of Education.*

In the years after *Brown* and the momentous civil rights movement it both reflected and encouraged, Mexican-Americans became even more active in their demands for equality and for the respect they deserved as American citizens. The Civil Rights Act of 1964 prohibited all public and much private discrimination or segregation "on the ground of race, color, religion, or national origin." The words "national origin" clearly included Mexican-Americans as well as other ethnic groups and helped raise public awareness of the fact that Mexican-Americans and other Latinos and Latinas were as much the objects of discrimination as were African-Americans.

That lesson made an impact on the Ford Foundation, which gave large grants to the NAACP in the 1960s. The NAACP Legal Defense and Education Fund offered to use some of the money to help Mexican-American lawyers in Texas with litigation. The Fund contacted Pete Tijerina, an attorney and former LULAC state civil rights chairman. Tijerina asked whether, instead of sending African-American lawyers to help Mexican-Americans, it might not be a better idea to create a Mexican-American version of the Fund. Jack Greenberg, the Fund's executive director, agreed to contact the Ford Foundation. In 1967–1968, with the help of a $2.2 million grant from Ford, the Mexican American Legal Defense and Education Fund (MALDEF) was born. Part of the grant was designated for the education of Mexican-American attorneys in the Southwest.

The creation of MALDEF was a crucial moment in the history of the struggle for Mexican-American equality. In the years before and after *Mendez*, there was no Mexican-American equivalent of the NAACP — no national organization with the funding and expertise to mount a systematic attack on segregation. As Guadalupe San Miguel Jr. has pointed out, "Mexican-American desegregation lawsuits . . . were the result of ad hoc, short-term legal strategies." Writing to Roger Baldwin in 1942 about Mexican-American desegregation efforts, George I. Sánchez lamented, "There is no organization that has ever assumed the sponsorship of these matters. These people are, institutionally, an orphan people. A few individuals like myself have been carrying the burden alone."

There were many reasons for the lack of organization, including both the relatively short time the overwhelming majority of Mexican-Americans had lived in the United States and the poverty of much of that population. As we have seen, although there was Mexican-American union organizing in the decades before LULAC was created in the late 1920s and before *Mendez*, the community as such was largely removed from the American political and legal arenas. The story of the NAACP and the African-American civil rights movement demonstrates that social movements are usually led by an elite within a discriminated-against group. Many of the African-American leaders in the early decades of the twentieth century were lawyers and ministers. The *Californios*, the Mexican-American elite that might have led a drive for racial equality, however, demonstrated little interest in the largely impoverished newcomers. With some exceptions, the Spanish-language newspapers in California focused primarily on local, nonpolitical issues such as marriages, divorces, and crops.

In addition, many immigrants from Mexico chose not to become American citizens. They planned to remain in the United States but opted to retain their Mexican citizenship, perhaps aware that they would be discriminated against no matter what their status. Some thought that becoming American citizens would constitute disloyalty to Mexico; others, who had entered the country illegally, would face deportation if they attempted to naturalize. Yet another reason for Mexican immigrants to keep their Mexican citizenship was that, as people with little recourse to the political system and even less faith in the ability of American law to benefit them, they could call on Mexican consuls for help. As the Lemon Grove case indicated, this access to Mexican consuls could be important. There were dozens of Mexican consular representatives in the United States, particularly in the Southwest, serving as organizers of Mexican communities, sponsors of Mexican Independence Day celebrations, and translators for local Anglo businesspeople. The consulate also supported the Sleepy Lagoon defense effort. As mentioned earlier, David Marcus worked for the Mexican consulate early in his career and still had a close relationship with it at the time of the case. Citizenship had not protected the many Mexican-Americans who were deported in the 1930s. Immigrants, particularly those who had not become American citizens, were more likely to rely on the consuls than on the American political or legal process. They stayed away from the courts and, with neither a substantial number of voters nor of political organizations, could exercise little political clout.

That, of course, changed when the American-born children of Mexican immigrants came to maturity and as a result of World War II. By the mid-1940s, there were more Mexican-Americans — those born in the United States of immigrant parents or of parents themselves born in the United States — than Mexican noncitizens living in the United States. Many of them were ready to become politically involved. The Unity Leagues they created have already been mentioned, and numerous other organizations sprang up as well. The Community Service Organization, created in East Los Angeles by Mexican-Americans in 1947, for example, emphasized voter registration and civic improvement. Activists were increasingly aware of other groups' struggles against discrimination. In May 1946, *La Opinión* ran a news story about Ku Klux Klan incidents in Los Angeles —

particularly notable because newsprint was still in short supply in the post–World War II United States, so newspapers had to pick and choose their stories carefully. The next month, the paper carried a large advertisement for a rally against the Ku Klux Klan, meant to protest the KKK's *actos de terrorismo* (acts of terrorism) against Catholics, Jews, and Negroes. The rally's organizers included African-American singer Lena Horne as well as Attorney General Robert Kenny. Mexican-Americans and African-Americans had begun to work together and to learn from each other.

The war did more than create a large number of Mexican-American veterans who understood what it was to fight for democracy and equality. As the Supreme Court's language in the *Hirabayashi* case and Kenny's brief in *Mendez* indicated, the war also helped stimulate new thinking about race and justice in the minds of the legal elite and other Americans. Most concerned Anglos, including that elite, assumed that the country's racial problems involved only the black-white divide. That remained true in much of the country, but not in the Southwest. There, educators were having doubts about the utility and fairness of segregation.

Foreign policy considerations also continued to affect attitudes. When the war ended and the Cold War began, the United States became concerned about possible communist penetration of Latin America and the votes of Latin American nations in the United Nations. Historians Mary Dudziak and Thomas Borstelmann have demonstrated that the Cold War and the competition between the Soviet Union and the United States for the hearts and minds of people around the world made American policy makers aware of the negative impact American racism had on international public opinion. While the policy makers and much of the world focused on black-white relations, the United States' interests in Mexico and other parts of Latin America made attitudes there of similar concern. President Harry S. Truman underscored the importance of Mexico to the United States in 1947 when he became the first American president to visit Mexico City and returned to the Mexican government some of the banners American troops had captured during the 1848 war. It had become vital to American policy makers to portray the United States as a place where people of Mexican ancestry were treated justly.

American governmental policy toward Mexico and Mexican-

Americans, in other words, paralleled and no doubt contributed to the elite's rethinking about the treatment of Mexican-Americans. That thinking was evident in the letters written by Judge Denman and Governor Warren. David Marcus was certainly aware of the international considerations, and perhaps Judge McCormick was as well. Marcus's passionate brief for the trial court had included the sentence "Eager eyes and attentive ears North and South of our borders await the result" of the case.

What all this suggests is that the *Mendez* case probably would not have succeeded had it been brought ten years earlier. Gilbert González has noted that "the California courts heard the *Mendez* case in a period of policy shift toward 'intercultural understanding,'" in which prejudice and discrimination had come to be seen as "negative social forces." There is an ongoing relationship between law and society, and societal attitudes had to change before a judge would write that segregation, with its implication of inferiority, was unjust or law reviews would publish articles calling for the overturning of *Plessy v. Ferguson*. Law, in turn, affects societal dynamics. *Mendez* clearly heartened the Mexican-American community and its activists, encouraging the spate of litigation and pressure on school boards that gradually ended segregation policies in many districts. In effect, *Mendez* validated and encouraged the efforts of individuals such as Gus García and Hector García as well as organizations such as AGIF and LULAC.

Mendez stimulated the Mexican-American community and gave it reason to believe that perhaps justice could be achieved in the United States. It directly affected the strategy used by the NAACP in *Brown v. Board of Education*. It helped delineate the scope of the Fourteenth Amendment, with Judge McCormick holding that the Constitution guaranteed Mexican-Americans the right to equality under the law. As Earl Warren did a decade later in *Hernandez*, McCormick interpreted the Fourteenth Amendment as being about more than the relationship of Anglos and African-Americans. And the case got the Méndez children, and other Mexican-American children in California, the education that enabled so many of them to become lawyers, judges, doctors, nurses, teachers, and legislators. For them, *Mendez* made the American dream a reality.

Epilogue

The Munemitsu family was able to return to Westminster in 1946, after the war ended. They worked side by side on the farm with the Méndezes for a few months so that Gonzalo and Felícitas could harvest the crop they had already planted and use the money to buy another café. The three Méndez children went to school at Westminster Main, which now housed all the district's children in grades one through four.

The Méndezes then reclaimed their Santa Ana home, moving there before the Ninth Circuit opinion was handed down. Santa Ana had not yet desegregated, but the Méndezes took their children to the local "white" school; officials there knew about the litigation and quietly enrolled them. Gonzalo and Felícitas opened a cantina in nearby Midway City. Sylvia went on to college and became a registered pediatric nurse. Jerome joined the armed forces and served as a Green Beret for many years; Gonzalo Jr. became a master carpenter.

David Marcus maintained his private practice almost until his death in 1982, continuing to handle a combination of civil liberties and other seemingly more glamorous matters. At one point he successfully fought a deportation order for actress Rita Hayworth's husband of the moment; at another, he was both the trial and state appeals court lawyer in a major search and seizure case (*Rochin v. California*, 1952) that was eventually taken to and won in the U.S. Supreme Court by A. L. Wirin. Tragically, Marcus was less successful in his battle against alcoholism, and he was disbarred for inadequate representation of clients two years before he died.

George Holden remained in the county counsel's office, where he occasionally found himself in somewhat unhappy contact with other *Mendez* attorneys. In 1954, while he was still deputy county counsel,

Holden questioned a Laguna Beach teacher who had refused to answer questions about Communist Party membership. She appeared at the hearing with her lawyer, Robert W. Kenny, the former attorney general who had been an amicus in the *Mendez* case. Kenny later became a California judge. Holden became county counsel in 1961. A year later he recommended the ouster of a Fullerton Junior College instructor and member of the Socialist Workers' Party who admitted to former membership in the Communist Party. The instructor's lawyers, who included A. L. Wirin and Fred Okrand, managed to have the ouster overturned by the California District Court of Appeals.

Judge McCormick, by then the sole Republican appointee among the ten federal judges in the Southern District as well as its chief judge, retired in September 1951 at age seventy-two. He was succeeded as chief judge by Leon Yankwich, who had decided the San Bernardino swimming pool case. Yankwich spoke at a 1961 ceremony in honor of McCormick, the year following McCormick's death. The main eulogy at that event was given by Judge John J. Ford, who said of McCormick, "He measured up to the conception of an ideal judge."

The Méndezes had two more children before Gonzalo, only fifty-one years old, died of heart failure in 1964. Felícitas, who died at age eighty-one, lived long enough to know that the Santa Ana Unified School District had broken ground for the new Gonzalo and Felicitas Mendez Fundamental Intermediate School. It opened in 2000. The farm the Méndezes and Munemitsus worked was eventually sold and, perhaps fittingly, became the grounds of Westminster's Finley Elementary and Johnson Intermediate Schools.

In 1998 the Los Angeles Board of Education issued a resolution commemorating the entire Méndez family. It was only one of many such resolutions, including those from the California legislature. When the U.S. Congress passed a resolution celebrating the fiftieth anniversary of *Brown v. Board of Education* in 2004, it acknowledged that the *Mendez* case "had successfully dismantled school segregation years before *Brown* . . . in Orange County." The House of Representatives passed a resolution in 2007, recognizing the sixtieth anniversary of the *Mendez* decision, honoring the Méndez family and Sylvia Méndez's role in teaching about it, and encouraging "the continued fight against school segregation."

California universities also began to take note of the case and its importance. In 2004 the University of California at Los Angeles held an all-day conference about *Mendez*. It was sponsored by the university's Chicano Studies Research Center, an institution that was of course not even dreamed of back in the 1940s. One of the events was the screening of *Mendez vs. Westminster: For All the Children/Para Todos los Niños*, a 2003 documentary that earned writer-producer Sandra Robbie an Emmy and a Golden Mike Award. Robbie and Michael Matsuda also wrote *Mendez vs. Westminster: For All the Children—An American Civil Rights Victory*, a children's book published in 2006. That same year, Chapman University held a program about the case. Ninety-three-year-old Josefina Ramírez, wife of one of the original plaintiffs in *Mendez*, was in the audience.

There was more recognition to come. In 2007 the U.S. Postal Service issued the stamp entitled "Mendez v. Westminster 1947: Toward Equality in Our Schools," which is reproduced on the cover of this volume. The idea for the stamp came from Maruchi Santana, a Cuban-born member of the Citizens' Stamp Advisory Committee that helps the Postal Service pick the images for commemorative stamps. The designer was Mexican-born Rafael López. His stamp portrays two young people reading a book, with darkness at their backs but sunshine ahead. It was officially unveiled on September 14, 2007, at the Gonzalo and Felicitas Mendez Fundamental Intermediate School. The Méndez family was there; so were members of the other plaintiffs' families, as well as the Vidaurri and Munemitsu families. The main speaker at the event was Thurgood Marshall Jr., a member of the U.S. Postal Service Board of Governors.

Paradoxically, even as the ceremony was taking place, the school desegregation for which the families had worked so hard had become more elusive than ever. There was no longer any legally mandated school segregation in California; *Mendez v. Westminster* and the act of the California legislature had seen to that. However, increasing urbanization in the 1960s and 1970s, and the movement of Mexican-Americans from rural districts into what became urban ethnic ghettoes, had created the new problem of de facto segregation—segregation that is not embodied in law but exists in fact. As of the first decade of the twenty-first century, the majority of Mexican-Americans—like far too many African-American students — were in segregated urban schools.

Gary Orfield and Chungmei Lee of UCLA's Civil Rights Project/ Proyecto Derechos Civiles reported that in 2006–2007, Latino students across the country attended schools in which more than half the students were Latinos. Ninety percent of Latino students in California were in such schools; 50 percent of them went to schools where Latinos made up 90 percent of the student body. "Too often Latino students face triple segregation by race, class, and language," Orfield and Lee noted. Urban and many suburban neighborhoods were largely segregated, and Mexican-American students attended class primarily with other Mexican-American students. Many of them were tracked into what amounted to segregated classes for supposed slow learners. The "commingling of the entire student body" about which Judge McCormick wrote, which "instills and develops a common cultural attitude among the school children which is imperative for the perpetuation of American institutions and ideals," was not taking place in those classrooms. Segregated schools, the judge had written, "foster antagonisms in the children and suggest inferiority among them where none exists." That had not changed.

In 2008 the California legislature passed a bill mandating the teaching of *Mendez* as part of the state's social studies curriculum. Governor Arnold Schwarzenegger vetoed the bill, in keeping with his opposition to the legislature's involvement in details of curriculum. The following year the California State Board of Education drafted a History–Social Science Curriculum Framework that included optional teaching about *Mendez* in the fourth grade and again in high school. The board was scheduled to vote on adopting the draft during the 2013–2014 school year.

In 1998, when Felícitas Méndez was terminally ill, she spoke with her daughter Sylvia about her regret that Gonzalo had died before the *Mendez* case became better known. Sylvia dedicated herself to educating the public about it. *Mendez* was an important moment in Mexican-American history, she would tell audiences, but it was equally significant as a moment when Mexican-Americans, African-Americans,

Japanese-Americans, and Jewish-Americans cooperated to undo what they saw as a great injustice. "*Mendez* is about everybody coming together," she commented in 2009.

And in *Mendez*, during those optimistic postwar years when it appeared that justice was close at hand and all things were possible, they did.

CASES CITED

Alvarez v. Lemon Grove School District, Superior Court of the State of California, County of San Diego, Petition for Writ of Mandate No. 66625, February 13, 1931

Berea College v. Commonwealth of Kentucky, 211 U.S. 45 (1908)

Brown v. Board of Education, 347 U.S. 483 (1954)

Cumming v. Board of Education, 175 U.S. 528 (1899)

Delgado v. Bastrop Independent School District, Civ. No. 388 (W.D. Tex. June 15, 1948)

Ex parte Endo, 323 U.S. 283 (1944)

Gong Lum v. Rice, 275 U.S. 78 (1927)

Gonzalez v. Sheely, 96 F. Supp. 1004 (D.C. Ariz. 1951)

Hernandez v. Texas, 347 U.S. 475 (1954)

Hirabayashi v. United States, 320 U.S. 81 (1943)

Kerr et al. v. Enoch Pratt Free Library of Baltimore City, 149 F.2d 212 (4th Cir. 1945), *cert. denied*, 326 U.S. 721 (1945)

Korematsu v. United States, 323 U.S. 214 (1944)

Lopez v. Seccombe, 71 F. Supp. 769 (S.D. Cal. 1944)

McLaurin v. Oklahoma State Regents, 339 U.S. 637 (1950)

Mendez v. Westminster School Dist. of Orange County, 64 F. Supp. 544 (C.D. Cal. 1946); *Westminster School Dist. of Orange County v. Mendez*, 161 F.2d 774 (9th Cir. 1947)

Meyer v. Nebraska, 262 U.S. 390 (1923)

Missouri ex rel. Gaines v. Canada, 305 U.S. 337 (1938)

Murray v. Pearson, 169 Md. 478 (1936)

Nixon v. Condon, 286 U.S. 73 (1932)

People v. Zamora, 66 Cal.App.2d 166 (1944) (Sleepy Lagoon case)

Plessy v. Ferguson, 163 U.S. 537 (1896)

Rochin v. California, 342 U.S. 165 (1952)

Salvatierra v. Del Rio Independent School District, 33 S.W.2d 790 (Tex. Civ. App., 1930); *cert. denied*, 284 U.S. 580 (1931)

Soria v. Oxnard School Dist. Bd. of Trustees, 386 F. Supp. 539 (C.D. Cal. 1974)

Sweatt v. Painter, 339 U.S. 629 (1950)

Tape v. Hurley, 66 Cal. 473 (1885)

Ward v. Flood, 48 Cal. 36 (1874)

West Virginia State Board of Education v. Barnette, 319 U.S. 624 (1943)

Yick Wo v. Hopkins, 118 U.S. 356 (1886)

CHRONOLOGY

1848	Treaty of Guadalupe Hidalgo is signed, ending the Mexican-American War and giving much of what became the American Southwest to the United States.
1869–1893	California enacts laws, subsequently amended, permitting school districts to segregate Asian and Indian students.
1876–1880, 1884–1911	Porfirio Díaz is president of Mexico.
1896	U.S. Supreme Court holds that "separate but equal" public accommodations are constitutional (*Plessy v. Ferguson*).
1910–1920	Mexican Revolution. Large-scale immigration from Mexico to the United States begins.
1910–1930	An estimated 1 million Mexicans migrate to the United States.
1913–1920s	"Mexican" schools are established in Southern California, including Orange County.
1919	Six-year-old Gonzalo Méndez and his family migrate to the United States.
1921, 1924	U.S. immigration laws sharply curtail immigration from Europe but not from Mexico or other Latin American nations.
1926	Felícitas Gómez (later Méndez) and her family move from Puerto Rico to the mainland.
1927	David Marcus graduates from law school and goes to work for the Mexican consulate.
1929	League of United Latin American Citizens (LULAC) is founded in Texas.
1929–1930s	An estimated half million Mexicans and Mexican-Americans are deported.
1930	U.S. Census Bureau announces that Mexicans will not be considered "white."
1930	LULAC and parents in Texas bring *Salvatierra v. Del Rio Independent School District*.
1931	Parents in Southern California bring *Alvarez v. Lemon Grove School District*.
1935	Gonzalo and Felícitas Méndez are married.
1936	Sylvia Méndez, the first of the Méndezes' children, is born.
1940	President Franklin D. Roosevelt creates Office of Inter-American Affairs; Division of Inter-American Activities is added in 1942.

1940–1945	Mexican-American parents in Westminster, Garden Grove, Santa Ana, and El Modena protest to school boards about segregated schools, to no avail.
1941–1945	Hundreds of thousands of Mexican-Americans serve in World War II.
1942–1943	*People v. Zamora* (Sleepy Lagoon case).
1943	Zoot Suit Riots in Los Angeles.
1943	Returning veterans create the Latin American Organization in Santa Ana.
1943	The Méndezes move to the Munemitsu farm in Westminster; Soledad Vidaurri tries to enroll the Méndez children in Westminster Main School.
1943	Mexican-Americans and David Marcus bring *Lopez v. Seccombe* (San Bernardino swimming pool case), which is decided in 1944.
March 2, 1945	David Marcus files *Mendez v. Westminster* in federal district court.
June 26, 1945	Pretrial hearing in *Mendez*.
July 5–11, 1945	Trial in *Mendez*.
February 18, 1946	Judge Paul McCormick hands down his decision in *Mendez*.
May 1946	LULAC chapter is organized in Orange County.
1946	Westminster integrates its elementary schools, and the Méndez children enroll in Westminster Main; the other three districts do not integrate. Schools are desegregated in Ontario, Riverside, and Indio. The Munemitsu family returns to Westminster. A few months later, the Méndezes move back to Santa Ana.
1946	NAACP, American Civil Liberties Union, American Jewish Congress, Japanese-American Citizens League, and California attorney general Robert W. Kenny join the *Mendez* case as amici.
December 9, 1946	*Mendez* is argued before the Ninth Circuit Court of Appeals.
January 1947	Bill to end segregated education in California is introduced in the California legislature; it is passed by the assembly in April and by the senate in June.
April 14, 1947	Ninth Circuit Court of Appeals hands down its decision in *Mendez*. Shortly thereafter, the school districts decide not to appeal further.

June 14, 1947	Governor Earl Warren signs school desegregation bill into law.
September 1947	Schools in Garden Grove, El Modena, and Santa Ana are desegregated.
1948	American GI Forum organized in Texas; ruling in *Delgado v. Bastrop Independent School District* desegregates schools in four south Texas districts.
1951	*Gonzalez v. Sheely* orders desegregation in an Arizona school district.
May 3, 1954	U.S. Supreme Court holds that Mexican-Americans are protected by the Fourteenth Amendment (*Hernandez v. Texas*); it rules two weeks later that school segregation is unconstitutional (*Brown v. Board of Education*).
1964	Gonzalo Méndez dies.
1967	Mexican American Legal Defense and Education Fund is created.
1998	Felícitas Méndez dies.
2000	Dedication of Gonzalo and Felicitas Mendez Fundamental Intermediate School in Santa Ana.
2007	U.S. Postal Service issues a stamp commemorating *Mendez v. Westminster.*

BIBLIOGRAPHICAL ESSAY

Note from the Series Editors: The following bibliographic essay contains the major primary and secondary sources the author consulted for this volume. We have asked all authors in the series to omit formal citations in order to make our volumes more readable, inexpensive, and appealing for students and general readers. In adopting this format, Landmark Law Cases and American Society follows the precedent of a number of highly regarded and widely consulted series.

Mexican-American History

There are a number of good introductions to Mexican-American history. Two useful places to start are David G. Gutiérrez, *Walls and Mirrors: Mexican Americans, Mexican Immigrants, and the Politics of Ethnicity* (University of California Press, 1995), and Gilbert G. González and Raul A. Fernandez, *A Century of Chicano History: Empire, Nations, and Migration* (Routledge, 2003). Juan Gómez-Quiñones, *Roots of Chicano Politics, 1600-1940* (University of New Mexico Press, 1994), tells the story up to the *Mendez* case. An earlier volume is Carey McWilliams, *North from Mexico* (Greenwood Press, 1948), written by the lawyer-activist who was prominent in the Sleepy Lagoon case. The book was updated in 1968, and an additional chapter was added by Matt S. Meier in 1989.

Gilbert G. González, *Labor and Community: Mexican Citrus Worker Villages in a Southern California County, 1900–1950* (University of Illinois Press, 1994), is about Orange County and describes the development of the citrus belt, working conditions, life in the *colonias*, unionization and strikes, and the rise of political organizations in the 1940s. It has a chapter on education. See also Gilbert G. González, *Guest Workers or Colonized Labor? Mexican Labor Migration to the United States* (Paradigm Publishers, 2006). George J. Sánchez, *Becoming Mexican American: Ethnicity, Culture, and Identity in Chicano Los Angeles, 1900–1945* (Oxford University Press, 1993), focuses on that city while depicting the history of Mexican immigration to the United States, Americanization efforts in California and elsewhere in the Southwest, Mexican-American labor activism, and the emergence of second-generation Mexican-Americans. Camille Guérin-Gonzalez, *Mexican Workers and American Dreams: Immigration, Repatriation, and California Farm Labor, 1900–1939* (Rutgers University Press, 1994), examines the history of Mexican immigrants in Southern California as well as the repatriation drive of the 1930s and the situation of California farm labor in the 1920s and 1930s. The epigraphs in chapters 1 and 3 are from Ruth D. Tuck, *Not with the Fist: Mexican-Americans in a South-*

west City (Harcourt Brace, 1946), xii, 187. The city of "Descanso" described in the book is actually San Bernardino. Gustavo Arellano's "Gunkist Oranges," a June 8, 2006, story in the *OC Weekly*, is about the 1936 citrus workers' strike. It is available at http://www.ocweekly.com/2006-06-08/news/gunkist-oranges/. See also Juan Gómez-Quiñones, *Mexican American Labor, 1790–1990* (University of New Mexico Press, 1994).

Vicki L. Ruiz, *From out of the Shadows: Mexican Women in Twentieth-Century America* (Oxford University Press, 1998), is the place to begin reading about women organizers. It also discusses labor organizing generally as well as mutual aid and other societies, starting with the early days of immigration and going through the Chicano-Chicana movement. The New Deal period is covered in Richard Griswold del Castillo, ed., *World War II and Mexican American Civil Rights* (University of Texas Press, 2008), a collection of essays and documents such as the executive order establishing the Fair Employment Practices Committee and affidavits describing discrimination in Texas during the war years. The statistics about service in World War II come from Latino Advocates for Education Inc. Mario T. García, *Mexican Americans: Leadership, Ideology, & Identity, 1930–1960* (Yale University Press, 1989), describes organizing in the 1940s and thereafter. Enrique M. López, "Community Resistance to Injustice and Inequality: Ontario, California, 1937–1947," 17 *Aztlán* 2 (1988), 1–29, tells the story of desegregation efforts in a Southern California community before and immediately after World War II.

Education of Mexican-Americans

Gilbert G. González, *Chicano Education in the Era of Segregation* (Balch Institute Press, 1990), covers Mexican-American education in the first half of the twentieth century. Richard R. Valencia, *Chicano Students and the Courts: The Mexican American Legal Struggle for Educational Equality* (New York University Press, 2008), has an opening chapter about the pre-*Mendez* cases and then discusses desegregation and integration efforts through the second half of the twentieth century. Nicolas C. Vaca, *The Presumed Alliance: The Unspoken Conflict between Latinos and Blacks and What It Means for America* (Rayo, 2004), considers segregated education in the Southwest generally and in Santa Ana specifically, as well as various educational theories. The summaries of educators' theories in chapter 1 are from Vaca and from the Wollenberg volume and the Arriola article cited below. José F. Moreno edited *The Elusive Quest for Equality: 150 Years of Chicano/Chicana Education* (*Harvard Educational Review*, 1999), which includes articles tracing education in the Southwest from before the Treaty of Guadalupe Hidalgo to 1998. Vicki L. Ruiz covers segregated schools in "South by Southwest: Mexican Americans and Segregated Schooling, 1900–1950," 15 *Organization of American History Magazine of History* (Winter 2001), available at http://www.oah.org/pubs/magazine/deseg/ruiz.html. Also see Ruben Donato, *The Other Struggle for Equal Schools* (State University of New York Press, 1997); Hershel T. Manuel, *The Education of Mexican and Spanish-Speaking Children in Texas* (University of Texas–Austin, Fund for Research in the Social Sciences, 1930); and Guadalupe San Miguel Jr., *"Let All of Them Take Heed": Mexican Americans and the Campaign for Educational Equality in Texas, 1910–1981* (University of Texas Press, 1987).

Charles M. Wollenberg's seminal *All Deliberate Speed: Segregation and Exclusion in California Schools, 1855–1975* (University of California Press, 1976) examines the segregation of African-Americans, Asian-Americans, and Native Americans as well as Mexican-Americans in California. It has a fine discussion of *Mendez* and of the educational theories first justifying and later attacking segregation (chap. 5), as does Wollenberg's *"Mendez v. Westminster*, Race, Nationality and Segregation in California Schools," 53 *California Historical Quarterly* 324 (Winter 1974). Mary M. Peters's "The Segregation of Mexican American Children in the Elementary Schools of California – Its Legal and Administrative Aspects" (master's thesis, UCLA, July 1948) draws on the experience of Ontario, California, and is a useful history of educational segregation as it existed in Southern California. The description of the Oxnard "Mexican" school in chapter 3 is in *Soria v. Oxnard School Dist. Bd. of Trustees*, 386 F. Supp. 539 (C.D. Cal. 1974).

Merton Earle Hill's dissertation that encouraged segregation, quoted in chapter 1, is "The Development of an Americanization Program" (Ed.D. dissertation, Graduate Division of the University of California, 1928). Grace Stanley's "Special School for Mexicans," cited in the same chapter, was in *The Survey*, September 15, 1920. Superintendent James L. Kent's thesis, introduced into evidence during the *Mendez* trial and quoted in chapter 5, is "Segregation of Mexican School Children in Southern California" (Ed.M. thesis, University of Oregon, 1941). *Education for Cultural Unity*, the Seventeenth Yearbook of the California Elementary School Principals' Association, was edited by N. D. Myers and published by the association in Oakland, California, in 1945.

Those interested in the years after the 1940s might look at Guadalupe Salinas, "Mexican Americans and the Desegregation of Schools in the Southwest," 8 *Houston Law Review* 929 (1971), and Kenneth J. Meier and Joseph Stewart Jr., *The Politics of Hispanic Education: UN Paso Pa'Lante Y DOS Pa'Tras* (SUNY, 1991), a comprehensive account of Hispanic education as of the end of the 1980s. The article by Gary Orfield and Chungmei Lee referred to in the epilogue is "Historic Reversals, Accelerating Resegregation, and the Need for New Integration Strategies" (UCLA, Civil Rights Project/Proyecto Derechos Civiles, August 2007). It is available at http://www.civilrightsproject.ucla .edu/research/deseg/reversals_eseg_need.pdf.

The transcript and other documents from the trial are in Case File CV-4299 (1945), *Gonzalo Mendez et al. v. Westminster School District of Orange, CA, et al.* (64 F. Supp. 544 [C.D. Cal. 1946]), available from the National Archives repository in Laguna Niguel, California. The statements by Mexican-American parents about their futile appeals to local school officials, quoted in chapter 3, come from the trial transcript. The Santa Ana school board minutes are quoted in González, *Chicano Education*, and the same author's "Segregation of Mexican Children in a Southern California City: The Legacy of Expansionism and the American Southwest," 16 *Western Historical Quarterly* 55 (January 1985); the El Modena minutes are in the Arriola files at Stanford University (see below); and the Garden Grove and Westminster minutes are quoted in the pretrial hearing and trial transcripts.

The appeals-level documents are held by the National Archives – Pacific Sierra Region in San Bruno, California, as *Westminster School District v. Mendez*, Case Files, Ninth Circuit Court of Appeals, Record Group 276, Box 4464 (161 F.2d 774 [9th Cir. 1947]).

Christopher J. Arriola has written a fine article on *Mendez:* "Knocking on the Schoolhouse Door: *Mendez v. Westminster*, Equal Protection, Public Education, and Mexican Americans in the 1940s," 8 *La Raza Law Journal* 166 (1995). Arriola did extensive research in archives and interviewed former Orange County students, including some of the participants in the case. He has deposited his materials with Special Collections at the Stanford University Library (however, for some inexplicable reason, the library does not permit photocopying of more than 10 percent of the collection). Judge Frederick P. Aguirre, "*Mendez v. Westminster School District:* How It Affected *Brown v. Board of Education*," 4 *Journal of Hispanic Higher Education* 321 (2005), is another solid article that discusses the case in depth. Its comparison of Judge McCormick's language with that of Justice Warren in *Brown v. Board of Education* is quoted in chapter 9. Vicki L. Ruiz's analysis of the case, which also draws the connection to *Brown*, is "We Always Tell Our Children They Are Americans: *Mendez v. Westminster* and the California Road to *Brown v. Board of Education*," 200 *College Board Review* (Fall 2003). Another version is in 6 *Brown Quarterly* (Fall 2004), at http://brownvboard.org/brwnqurt/06-3/.

The connection between *Mendez* and *Brown* is limned as well in Thomas A. Saenz, "*Mendez* and the Legacy of *Brown:* A Latino Civil Rights Lawyer's Assessment," *Berkeley Women's Law Journal* 395 (2004), and Richard Valencia, "The Mexican American Struggle for Equal Educational Opportunity in *Mendez v. Westminster:* Helping to Pave the Way for *Brown v. The Board of Education*," 107 *Teacher's College Record* (March 2005). Guadalupe San Miguel Jr. traces the relationship between *Brown* and later cases in "The Impact of *Brown* on Mexican American Desegregation Litigation, 1950s to 1980s," 4 *Journal of Latinos and Education* 221 (2005). Ed Cray is one of the few biographers of Earl Warren to mention *Mendez*. He does so in *Chief Justice: A Biography of Earl Warren* (Simon & Schuster, 1997). Carlos Haro and Nadine Bermudez were the coordinators for the UCLA Chicano Studies Research Center's "Symposium: *Mendez v. Westminster School District:* Paving the Path for School Desegregation and *Brown v. Board of Education*" (UCLA Chicano Studies Research Center, 2004). It is at http://www.chicano.ucla.edu/center/events/mendez_052104/052104_mendez.pdf.

The *Orange Daily News*, archived in a number of California libraries, carried articles about the case in 1945–1947. The *New York Times* articles, written by Lawrence E. Davies, were "Pupil Segregation on Coast Is Fought," December 10, 1946, and "Segregation of Mexican American Students Stirs Court Fight," *New York Times Magazine*, December 22, 1946. Carey McWilliams's article about the case was "Is Your Name Gonzales?" *Nation*, March 15, 1947. Drew Pearson's "Judge Denman Flails Anti-Mexican Discrimination," part of the "Washington Merry-Go-Round" column of May 11, 1947, is in the American University Archives and Special Collections and is available through the Washington Research Library Consortium at http://www.aladin.wrlc.org/gsdl/collect/pearson/pearson.shtml. *El Espectador* is archived in the Department of Special Collections at the Stanford University Libraries. Back issues of *La Opinión* are in the Young Research Library Microform and Media Service of the UCLA Library.

There is a 2002 documentary about *Mendez* entitled *Mendez vs. Westminster: For All the Children/Para Todos los Niños*, made by Sandra Robbie. She and Michael Matsuda also authored *Mendez vs. Westminster: For All the Children—An American Civil Rights Victory*, a children's book published by Blue State Press in 2006.

Anonymous law review articles that commented on the case were "Recent Cases — Constitutional Law — Equal Protection of the Laws," 30 *Minnesota Law Review* 646 (1945–1946); "Note, Segregation in Public Schools — A Violation of 'Equal Protection of the Laws,'" 56 *Yale Law Journal* 1059 (1947); "Note, Equal Protection of the Laws," 60 *Harvard Law Review* 1156 (September 1947); and "Note: Is Racial Segregation Consistent with Equal Protection of the Laws?" 49 *Columbia Law Review* 629 (May 1949). Bylined articles included Harry L. Gershon, "Comments: Restrictive Covenants and Equal Protection," 21 *Southern Columbia Law Review* 358 (1947–1948), and Neal Seegert, "Comment," 46 *Michigan Law Review* 639 (March 1948). The Clark Atlanta University articles mentioned in chapter 9 are Lester H. Phillips, "Segregation in Education: A California Case Study," 10 *Phylon: The Atlanta University Review of Race and Culture* 407 (1949), and Ira De A. Reid, "Persons and Places," 7 *Phylon* 197 (1946).

Other Cases

Robert R. Alvarez Jr., whose father was the lead plaintiff in the Lemon Grove case that preceded *Mendez*, tells the story in "The Lemon Grove Incident: The Nation's First Successful Desegregation Court Case," 32 *Journal of San Diego History* (1986), available at http://www.sandiegohistory.org/journal/ 86spring/lemongrove.htm. The case is dramatized in producer-writer Paul Espinosa's *The Lemon Grove Incident*, a docudrama produced by KPBS (San Diego) in 1985. There is another account of the case by Vicki L. Ruiz, "*Alvarez v. Lemon Grove*," in Vicki L. Ruiz and Virginia Sanchez Korrol, eds., *Latinas in the United States: A Historical Encyclopedia* (Indiana University Press, 2006), 45–46. The *Del Rio* case is described in Guadalupe San Miguel Jr., "The Struggle against Separate and Unequal Schools: Middle Class Mexican Americans and the Desegregation Campaign in Texas, 1929–1957," 23 *History of Education Quarterly* 343 (1983). Ricardo Romo examines the Sleepy Lagoon case, as well as *Mendez*, in "Southern California and the Origins of Latino Civil Rights Activism," 3 *Western Legal History* 379 (Summer/Fall 1990). Eduardo Obregón Pagán, *Murder at the Sleepy Lagoon: Zoot Suits, Race, & Riot in Wartime L.A.* (University of North Carolina Press, 2003), is a highly nuanced analysis of the Zoot Suit Riots and the social causes of the reaction to the Sleepy Lagoon case. Both text describing and pictures showing the zoot suiters are available in Dan Luckenbill, *The Pachuco Era* (1990), a catalog prepared for an exhibit at the UCLA Research Library, Department of Special Collections. It is accessible at http://www.library.ucla.edu/libraries/special/images/sleepy lagoon/pachuco.pdf. James A. Ferg-Cadima, "Black, White and Brown: Latino School Desegregation Efforts in the Pre– and Post–*Brown v. Board of Education* Era" (May 2004), is a short article by a MALDEF attorney; it is accessible at http://www.maldef.org/publications/pdf/LatinoDesegregation Paper2004.pdf. Also see Valencia, *Chicano Students and the Courts*, cited above, and Jeanne M. Powers and Lirio Patton, "Between *Mendez* and *Brown*: *Gonzales v. Sheely* (1951) and the Legal Campaign against Segregation," 33 *Law and Social Inquiry* 127 (Winter 2008), which places *Mendez*, *Delgado* and *Gonzalez* in the context of changing cultural norms. Clare Sheridan, " 'Another White Race': Mexican Americans and the Paradox of Whiteness in Jury Selection," 21 *Law and History Review* 109 (Spring 2003), is about the *Hernandez* case; it is available at http://www.historycooperative.org/journals/lhr/21.1/forum _sheridan.html.

Mexican-American Civil Rights Organizations

The history of LULAC is traced in Edward D. Garza, *LULAC: League of United Latin American Citizens* (R and E Research Associates, 1972); Benjamin

Márquez, *LULAC: The Evolution of a Mexican American Political Organization* (University of Texas Press, 1993); and Craig A. Kaplowitz, *LULAC, Mexican Americans and National Policy* (Texas A&M University Press, 2005). San Miguel's "The Struggle against Separate and Unequal Schools," cited earlier, has substantial information about both LULAC and other Mexican-American organizations. LULAC is also discussed in chapter 1 of García, *Mexican Americans: Leadership, Ideology, & Identity*, mentioned above. Margie de la Torre Aguirre, a LULAC activist in Yorba Linda, California, self-published a 2009 volume with photographs and documents. It is *LULAC Project: Patriots with Civil Rights, Early History of the League of United Latin American Citizens in California (1929–1957)*.

Two useful volumes about the American GI Forum are Carl Allsup, *The American G.I. Forum: Origins and Evolution*, Monograph 6 (University of Texas Center for Mexican American Studies, 1982), and Henry A. J. Ramos, *The American GI Forum: In Pursuit of the Dream, 1948–1983* (Arte Público Press, 1998). See also Carl Allsup, "Education Is Our Freedom: The American G.I. Forum and the Mexican American School Segregation in Texas, 1948–1957," 8 *Aztlán: A Journal of Chicano Studies* 27 (1977).

The origins of MALDEF are discussed in Maggie Rivas-Rodriguez and Maro Robbins, " 'To Have Our Own Lawyers Fight Our Own Cases': The Origins of the Mexican American Legal Defense and Educational Fund," an interview with Pete Tijerina, MALDEF's first executive director. It is available at http://historymatters.gmu.edu/d/6585/. Maurilio Vigil, "The Ethnic Organization as an Instrument of Political and Social Change: MALDEF, a Case Study," is in Manuel G. Gonzales and Cynthia M. Gonzales, eds., *En Aquel Entonces—In Years Gone By: Readings in Mexican-American History* (Indiana University Press, 2000). An earlier version with the same title is in 18 *Journal of Ethnic Studies* 15 (Spring 1990). See also Guadalupe San Miguel Jr., "Mexican American Organizations and the Changing Politics of School Desegregation in Texas, 1945–1980," 63 *Social Science Quarterly* 701 (1982).

The NAACP and Other Civil Rights Organizations

The history of the NAACP's struggle to desegregate schools has been recounted in many volumes, among them Mark Tushnet, *The NAACP's Legal Strategy against Segregated Education, 1925–1950* (University of North Carolina Press, 1987); Patricia Sullivan, *Lift Every Voice: The NAACP and the Making of the Civil Rights Movement* (New Press, 2009); Richard Kluger, *Simple Justice: The History of* Brown v. Board of Education *and Black America's Struggle for Equality* (Knopf, 1975, 2004); and Michael Klarman, *From Jim Crow to Civil Rights: The Supreme Court and the Struggle for Racial Equality* (Oxford University Press, 2004). Judge Robert L. Carter described his experiences as an NAACP attorney in "Re-examining *Brown* Twenty Five Years Later: Looking Backward into the Future," 14 *Harvard Civil Rights Civil Liberties Law Review* 615 (1979). The article by Judge Constance Baker Motley referred to in chapter 4 is "Standing on His Shoulders: Thurgood Marshall's Early Career," 35 *Howard Law Journal* 32 (1991). Also see Julius L. Chambers, "Thurgood Marshall's Legacy," 44 *Stanford Law Review* 1249 (Summer 1992). The NAACP papers, including much of Marshall's correspondence, are in the Library of Congress. So are the papers of the NAACP Legal Defense and Educational Fund, but unfortunately, the Fund makes it almost impossible for scholars to use them.

Samuel Walker's *In Defense of American Liberties: A History of the ACLU* (Southern Illinois University Press, 1999) is a good introduction to the ACLU. The correspondence between Roger Baldwin of the ACLU and George I. Sánchez is in Box 2, Folders 17–20, of the George I. Sánchez Papers at the Nettie Lee Benson Latin American Collection, University of Texas Libraries at Austin. The history of the National Lawyers Guild is detailed in Ann Fagan Ginger and Eugene M. Tobin, eds., *The National Lawyers Guild: From Roosevelt through Reagan* (Temple University Press, 1988). Chapter 4 of Stuart Svonkin's *Jews against Prejudice: American Jews and the Fight for Civil Liberties* (Columbia University Press, 1997) is about the American Jewish Congress's Commission on Law and Social Action, and Max Ascoli, "Alexander H. Pekelis, 1902–1946," 14 *Social Research* 2 (March 1947), is a good introduction to Pekelis's career. Material about the Japanese-American Citizens League is limited, but one place to start is Bill Hosokawa, *JACL in Quest of Justice* (William Morrow, 1982). The amicus briefs of the various organizations in *Mendez* are part of the case file in the National Archives in San Bruno mentioned above.

Biographic Information

Much of the information in this volume about the Méndez family came from Sylvia Méndez and from Gonzalo Méndez's testimony at trial. Professor Gilbert González interviewed Felícitas Méndez in the 1980s and used that material in *Chicano Education in the Era of Segregation*, cited above. See also Arriola, "Knocking on the Schoolhouse Door," cited above, and Jennifer McCormick and César J. Ayala, "Felícita 'La Prieta' Méndez (1916–1998) and the End of Latino School Segregation in California," 19 *CENTRO Journal* 13 (Fall 2007).

Information about David Marcus and his family was supplied by members of the Marcus family, particularly Professor Karen Melissa Marcus, and is also available in the *Los Angeles Times* and the records of the California Supreme Court, 1929–1979. The disbarment order was confirmed by that court in *David C. Marcus v. The State Bar of California*, 27 Cal. 3d 199; 611 P.2d 462; 165

Cal. Rptr. 121 (June 5, 1980). There is information about George Holden in various issues of the *Los Angeles Times*, 1938–1964, as well as in the files of the Orange County Public Library, Orange County Counsel, Orange County Archives, and Santa Ana History Rooms. Additional material came from Holden's sons Daniel W. Holden and Stephen Holden.

Judge McCormick's career was documented by the *Los Angeles Times*, 1908–1969; the *New York Times*, 1925 (Teapot Dome) and 1930–1933 (Wickersham Commission); and the *Biographical Directory of Federal Judges*, maintained by the Federal Judicial Center. That directory can be found at http://www .fjc.gov/public/home.nsf/hisj. It also contains data on Ninth Circuit Court judges Albert Lee Stephens and William Denman. Judge Denman's papers are archived at the library of the University of California at Berkeley, and the online biography that is part of the guide to those papers is at http://content .cdlib.org/view?docId=tf729005jo&chunk.id=bioghist-1.3.4&brand=oac. The San Francisco County Biographies also has a short biography of Denman, published in 1913, at http://freepages.genealogy.rootsweb.ancestry.com/ ~npmelton/sfbdenma.htm. There is a somewhat longer biography of Judge Stephens on the Web site of the California courts at http://www.courtinfo .ca.gov/courts/courtsofappeal/2ndDistrict/justices/former/StephensA.pdf.

Judge Leon R. Yankwich's career was followed by the *Los Angeles Times* in various articles published throughout his career. His book, referred to in chapter 3, is *The Constitution and the Future* (Graphic Press, 1936).

The Foreign Policy Component

The connection between domestic policy on racial issues and the United States' image abroad is covered in Emilio Zamora, *Claiming Rights and Righting Wrongs in Texas: Mexican Workers and Job Politics during World War II* (Texas A&M University Press, 2009), chap. 3, and in the aforementioned González, *Chicano Education in the Era of Segregation*, chap. 6. González's "Segregation of Mexican Children in a Southern California City," cited above, is the source of the quote about the political climate at the time of the *Mendez* case.

There are two solid volumes on the relationship between domestic and foreign policy in the mid-twentieth century, although they do not reference the U.S.-Mexico or U.S.–Latin America relationship. They are Mary L. Dudziak, *Cold War Civil Rights: Race and the Image of American Democracy* (Princeton University Press, 2000), and Thomas Borstelmann, *The Cold War and the Color Line: American Race Relations in the Global Arena* (Harvard University Press, 2001).

Whiteness

The issue of "whiteness" is too complicated to address fully in this volume. Jeanne M. Powers, "*Mendez v. Westminster* (1946) as a Window into Mid-Century Racial Ideologies," is available at http://www.allacademic.com// meta/p_mla_apa_research_citation/1/8/4/9/5/pages184950/p184950-1 .php. The topic is addressed in the context of Latinos in Mario García, *Mexican Americans: Leadership, Ideology, and Identity, 1930–1960* (Yale University Press, 1989); Ian F. Haney Lopez, "White Latinos," 6 *Harvard Latino Law Review* 2 (2003); and *Racism on Trial: the Chicano Fight for Justice* (Harvard University, 2003), which differentiates between Mexican-Americans and Chicanos; Carlos K. Blanton, "George I. Sánchez, Ideology, and Whiteness in the Making of the Mexican American Civil Rights Movement, 1930–1960," 72 *Journal of Southern History* 569 (2006); Neil Foley, "Becoming Hispanic: Mexican Americans and the Faustian Pact with Whiteness," in Neil Foley, ed., *Reflexiones 1997: New Directions in Mexican American Studies* (University of Texas at Austin, 1998); and Steven H. Wilson, "Brown over Other White: Mexican Americans' Legal Arguments and Litigation Strategy in School Desegregation Lawsuits," 21 *Law and History Review* 145 (Spring 2003), available at http://www.historycooperative.org/journals/lhr/21.1/forum_wilson .html. There is a good short history of the construction of whiteness in John Tehranian, *Whitewashed: America's Invisible Middle Eastern Minority* (New York University Press, 2009), chap. 1. Ian F. Haney Lopez, *White by Law: The Legal Construction of Race* (New York University Press, 1996), is a more extensive examination of the subject. See also Ariela J. Gross, "Litigating Whiteness: Trials of Racial Determination in the Nineteenth-Century South," 108 *Yale Law Journal* 117 (1998).

INDEX